PHIL STACEY
with THOMAS JEFFRIES

MADE TO WORSHIP

Empty Idols and the Fullness of God

Tyndale House Publishers
Carol Stream, Illinois

A Focus on the Family Resource
Published by Tyndale House Publishers

CONTENTS

INTRODUCTION

I'M BACKSTAGE on the set of *American Idol*, and I am absolutely terrified. Tens of millions will be watching tonight's live show, and my nerves are shot. Simply breathing is difficult. I'm sweating, and my legs are trembling.

I softly sing a Rich Mullins classic—"Hold me Jesus, 'cause I'm shaking like a leaf."

In a few minutes I will be escorted to the *Idol* stage to perform. While I'm waiting I wonder, *Why in the world have I gotten myself into this? All my dreams are right in front of me, but one misstep could cost me everything.*

The pressure has been building steadily, to the point where I'm having borderline panic attacks before each show. It's been this way for a few weeks now, and it's not getting any better.

Finally, the most wonderful woman in the world decides she's seen enough. My wife looks at me with all the love she can muster. The conversation goes something like this:

"Phil, you need to know that this is pride," Kendra says.

"It's eating away at you, and you need to get rid of it or it will destroy you."

I'm perplexed. "If this were pride," I reply, "I'd have at least some measure of confidence. What you're seeing right now is humility!"

"No, Phil. This is you being worried about how you come across on television because you want everyone to think you're good. But this isn't about you. There were thousands of auditions this year, and most of them were good. But those other singers aren't here. You are. And I imagine the only way that's possible is because God has prepared a way for you to be here.

"Seems to me that He has a purpose in all this. Seems to me that it's in His hands. And if you can fully trust Him, you'll stop worrying about how good you look and just start enjoying the ride. If you get eliminated, God has opened doors for you. If you make it through, God has opened doors for you. Either way, God will give you the grace to do whatever's necessary to accomplish His purpose."

Not only was Kendra right, her words immediately gave me a sense of peace. It wasn't about me. I'd bought into the idea that I was born for this, that this was my big shot. But my life was not in the hands of the *American Idol* judges—Simon Cowell, Randy Jackson, and Paula Abdul. My life was not in the hands of the millions of viewers—voters!—tuning in at home. My life was in the hands of a loving heavenly Father who was fully capable of giving me supernatural singing abilities if He chose to do so. He was also capable of extending my run for no other reason than to use my *Idol* experience for *His* glory.

I know that He did use me. I received countless messages from *Idol* fans telling me how one performance or another moved them in some way. But my favorite message had very little to do with me.

The woman who wrote to me was a Navy wife. She and her husband were on the brink of divorce, and one of the few times the two of them were in the same room together, they were watching *American Idol*. Since I was also in the Navy at the time, she was rooting for me. Unfortunately, this particular episode was not one of my best moments. It was actually quite terrible. She recalled how Simon Cowell was dumbfounded by my whole performance.

That's when an *Idol* camera focused on a woman in the audience. Kendra has a beautiful smile, and apparently she was beaming as she made eye contact with me from the crowd. The image cut back to me, but I wasn't looking at Simon while he delivered his critique. Instead, I was staring right at Kendra, which brought a smile to my face as well.

The Navy wife described feeling an overwhelming presence of love. She began to cry. Later that night, having looked me up online, she discovered I was a part-time worship leader. Strangely, it was her husband who first commented on the connection they'd witnessed between Kendra and me that night. That special connection, she told her husband, was because we had put God first in our relationship. After a conversation about how badly they both wanted their marriage to work, the couple made the decision to look for a Christian counselor and give their marriage one more try.

She told me that they had both committed their lives to Christ and had started attending a church close to their home. She said their marriage was reborn as they actively pursued a love built not on selfishness but on a foundation of faith. At the time I was probably more concerned about my lackluster singing, but God had done something special with that couple. God can create beauty from ashes, whether it's a poor performance on *American Idol* or a rough few years in a dying marriage. He can work all things together for our good.

Her message moved me immensely. *Even when I'm at my worst, God is still able to use me!* How liberating is that? It takes the pressure of a perfect performance off of my shoulders. My purpose isn't to entertain people or somehow manipulate them through the power of my vocal prowess. It's to bring glory to God.

I'm not a singer. I'm a worshiper. When I place what little I have in God's hands, He takes it, blesses it, and uses it far beyond my wildest expectations.

———

I wish I could say that this couple's story transformed my attitude completely. I can't. I wish I could say that the rest of my experience with the show was positive and uplifting. It wasn't. I wish I could say that I performed on *American Idol* for my children. I didn't.

I did it for myself.

I'd wanted to be a singer my whole life, and I spent more time away from my kids during that year than I spent with them. My message on *Idol* was "I want to encourage my kids to pursue their dreams." I don't know if they actually aired that comment on the show. They might have. But the truth is that I said that stuff when they stuck a television camera in my face because I thought it sounded good.

When you achieve your dreams, they're rarely as fulfilling as you thought they'd be. Then you dream new dreams, and when you attain those, they're still not as fulfilling as you hoped.

So finally, as believers, we come to the point where we find our fulfillment in Jesus Christ. Period. When God opens the doors, we experience genuine fulfillment. It doesn't matter how hard we fight to break through a wall, we are not going to feel truly fulfilled unless Christ is involved.

That's how I look back on *American Idol*. I went off the rails spiritually during that time. The year I was on *Idol* was not a good year for my marriage. It was not a good year for my kids. It was not a good year for any of my friendships.

It's hard to explain this to people who don't know Christ. After all, my dreams were coming true. I was making a lot of money, because they paid contestants to be on the show and then paid us even more to be on the *Idol* concert tour. After that, I signed a recording contract with a big advance check.

I was getting everything I ever wanted. I stayed in five-star hotels. I traveled around the country in a luxury bus. I enjoyed catered meals everywhere I went. You'd have thought my life was perfect; instead, it almost fell apart.

This is my story.

CHAPTER 1

GROWING UP

PEOPLE ASK ME if I remember performing music growing up. The truth is that I remember very little else.

I didn't do well in school. I wasn't good at making friends. I *was* good at music. In my house, my brother, sister, and I were challenged—and we were *rewarded*—when we learned new songs. We all took piano lessons; we all performed. My dad was a pastor, so he always had us kids singing onstage at church. We performed as individuals, in duets, and in trios. We gave out audio tapes of us singing as Christmas gifts.

Singing was like speaking in our house. Music was my life.

I arrived into the world on January 21, 1978, as Joel Philip Stacey, the third child of Gary and Adrell. I don't remember when it first happened, but I've always been called Phil. Everywhere I've moved since I was a child, I've tried to get people to start calling me Joel. If you watch my *American Idol* audition, you can hear Simon Cowell refer to me as Joel, but host Ryan Seacrest called me Phil and that was that.

I was born in Harlan County, Kentucky. Harlan County was a coal-mining area, and my dad was a Church of God pastor. We come from a long line of coal miners, preachers, farmers, and musicians. Both sides of my family are from pioneer-day Kentucky. I never watched it, but there was a popular television show called *Justified* that was based on the city of Harlan. They still make moonshine there—it's that kind of town.

My father wasn't always a preacher. He was the son of a preacher, and he went to Lee College, a Christian college, in the mid-1960s. Dad's life was kind of derailed during the Vietnam War era. The details are cloudy, because there are still things he won't talk to me about.

For a time in the late 1960s he was AWOL from the military, and it was during this period that he tried to become a professional musician. He played keyboards and trumpet in Chicago, Illinois, and connected with some really big stars at the time. But eventually, when he had run out of gigs and options, he turned himself in to the local police.

After my father served his time and fulfilled the rest of his enlistment, he actually tried to become a career military guy. "No," they said, "we don't need you." My dad is a patriot; he always has been. I guess I would call him a hippie patriot.

Vietnam was traumatic for him. He's told me a few stories. In one of them his company heard rustling in the leaves. They all simultaneously turned their M16s toward the noise and started firing. When the dust cleared, there were a million pieces of bunny rabbit all over the place. "That describes Vietnam," my father said. "Every single sound, every little impulse, was terrifying."

His typical response to questions I asked when I was younger was that anything that happened before he got saved didn't matter. He was born in 1945, but he says his life truly began when he surrendered his life to Christ in 1971. He eventually met my mom, returned to Lee College (today it's Lee University), graduated, and became a minister. He served first as a music minister, and then as an associate pastor, and then he started pastoring churches of his own. The Harlan County church was his first lead pastor role.

My father is a great musician. He's skilled at both the trumpet and piano, and he has a brilliant musical mind. He served on music boards in the church, and he wrote lots of convention songs and modern hymns. My father also sang. He would never call himself a singer because he was a band guy first, but he had a beautiful voice and, more importantly, a very emotional voice. A dramatic voice.

When I was a kid, I was sitting in church while Dad sang an old song called "The Day He Wore My Crown." (Sandi Patty later recorded it.) I just bawled. I was five or six years old, and I cried because Dad's performance was so emotionally powerful. It was a landmark moment for me, because it was when I first recognized music's strong influence on people.

My mother, Adrell, was born in 1953 in Neon, Kentucky—another region full of coal-mining towns. She was also raised in a pastor's home. In a pastor's home, there's always a lot of pressure, and my mother and her siblings definitely weren't immune. In spite of this, she grew up with a love and passion for ministry and used the incredible voice God gave her to sing and minister all over Kentucky.

Gary met Adrell while he was playing the piano at a camp meeting in Kentucky, which is like a regional spiritual revival. They were married in 1973.

My older brother, Keith, was born in 1975 in Cleveland, Tennessee. By the time my sister, Rebecca, arrived in 1976, the family had moved to a fishing village in Maryland. My father had various ministry jobs that took the family from place to place—all of them with the Church of God. My parents are Church of God through and through. Both of their parents were Church of God pastors. You know how some folks are dedicated, die-hard fans of their favorite sports team? That's the way it was with denominations. There was even a song with lyrics that said, "The Church of God is right, hallelujah to the Lamb." Yep, that was a song people really sang!

My siblings and I sang songs from convention books. You could walk into any church in Ohio or Kentucky, open these convention books, and see Dad's twenty or so songwriting credits. These books were the equivalent of our modern hymnals. We would thumb through them just to see how many songs Dad had written. You found them in Baptist churches, Assembly of God churches, and many others, but they were published by the Church of God publishing house. The denomination printed the red-back hymnals, and they were everywhere.

The Church of God always was—and still is—known for its music. On *The Voice* or *American Idol* or any of these other singing competitions, you'll often see people from the Church of God who have done well. If they're like me, they were raised in a musical environment. My mother grew up singing in church, and she was spectacular. She would *floor* people when she performed.

My mother's side of the family is overflowing with musical talent. Our family reunions always looked like a "Gaither Homecoming." At a certain point, everybody pulled out their musical instruments. We have a Julliard graduate who's played with the New York Philharmonic, and several people have toured musically around the country. Two of my uncles played guitar—both of them just bad to the bone—and my dad was on the keyboard. And then there were all these singers, basically a giant family choir.

My grandparents on that side had nine kids, and all of my mom's siblings had families, so family reunions included at least fifty people. When they'd start to jam, it was all gospel music—100 percent old hymns. When Dad got saved, he stopped playing secular music, because there was this idea in the church that anything other than gospel music was evil— an idea that was around until probably 1990.

My brother and sister and I were products of this musical environment. We were featured at the family reunions, along with all the other families' kids, and we all sang. Every one of the families had trios or duets, depending on how many kids they had. To me, there was a palpable sense of competition. My cousins inspired me to work harder and get better.

By the time I turned eight, I was already writing songs. I'm not saying I was a good songwriter back then. It's just who we were as a family. It wasn't that I was simply passionate about music—music was everything. For me, I can't remember a time *without* singing.

There are photos of me in my diaper up in front of a church, with one hand raised and a microphone in the other. I was probably singing "Jesus Loves Me" or something. It's ridiculous, but it was real. At that age you're barely learning vowels; you're not learning words. You have no idea what you're singing; you're just repeating what you've been taught to do.

One of my earliest memories involves my mother in

church. I was around three or four years old, and I can picture Mom standing next to me, clapping her hands and singing along to the old red-back hymnal. The year was 1981, and we were living in Pinsonfork, Kentucky.

The memory is as grainy as an old photo. The church had a small sanctuary with red carpet and wooden pews. Men wore suits; women wore dresses and big buns in their hair. It was a charming church filled with salt-of-the-earth type people. An old man named J.J. Phillips used to give the kids Red Hots candies every Sunday. He was a descendant of "Bad Frank" Phillips, the infamous deputy sheriff from the bitter Hatfield and McCoy feud that had plagued the area so many years before.

I remember an intense moment of learning on one particular Sunday. In fact, it could have been the moment I really learned how to sing. My mom was lifting her hands, and I joined her by lifting my hand. I remember watching her sing and watching people respond, because she couldn't sing without people standing up all over the congregation.

Not only that, but audiences were genuinely *moved* when my mother sang—crying, all that stuff—and it was profound. I witnessed the impact that her voice had on people. I didn't understand it yet, because I didn't understand the emotions. I didn't understand that there were stories in every one of those pews. I didn't understand that she was ministering spiritually, but I could see that the congregation was affected.

Mom was standing to my right, belting out the alto line with all her might. Her voice was mesmerizing, perfectly fit for a choir of angels. I stood next to her trying to mimic the way she sounded. I found myself using vibrato and learning to complement the melody of a song with a harmony line.

I was hooked.

CHAPTER 2

MOVING ON

IN 1982 OUR FAMILY MOVED from Pinsonfork, Kentucky, to Hamilton, Ohio—near Cincinnati—and that's where we stayed for the next ten years. We thrived musically in Ohio. It was a musical community with loads of young talent.

My earliest memories all involve music, so while I can't remember many specifics, I can tell you the songs we sang. I remember spending hours in the church recording our Christmas tapes. We recorded classic songs made popular by artists including Larnelle Harris and Sandi Patty. For example, I sang "How Majestic Is Your Name," and Rebecca sang "The Warrior Is a Child" by Twila Paris.

When I was first introduced to music, it wasn't described

as entertainment or a way to make a living. It was something profound and extraordinary. It was a gift. Here is this God who can breathe stars and planets into existence, and one thing He craves is our song. Scripture compels us sixty-four times to sing. It's among the Lord's most requested gifts from His people.

What made me fall in love with singing was not just the sound of it, but the way it made me feel. Specifically, *who* it made me feel. I actually felt the joy of the Lord when I sang. I could perceive God's presence enjoying my song. I could stand before a crowd and sense God's love for an audience filled with people I'd never met.

My siblings and I sang solos and we sang together. We won musical competitions. If I was competing as a male soloist, Rebecca was competing as a female soloist. Keith usually entered the instrumental category on piano. And we won a lot.

We practiced in the living room with Mom as our tutor and taskmaster. My mother is a sweet, amazing lady, but she was fierce in those practices. She was fierce when we performed. We'd be onstage while she coached us from the front row. She was like a baseball coach giving us signals—we knew exactly what she was communicating without her saying a word. If she lifted her eyebrows, it was our pitch. If she sat up straight and tall, it was our posture. If she smiled real big, we needed to smile. She was a great teacher. When my mother sang, people responded, and she trained us to reach an audience the same way.

There are a lot of great singers, she said, but the difference between the good singers and the best ones is the way they communicate. She taught us that when people attend a concert or any musical experience, most of what they take in is through their eyes, not their ears—so she focused on the visual: If you look nervous, you're giving your audience permission to be nervous. If you smile, you're giving your audience permission to smile. Whatever we did onstage, we gave the church permission to do the same thing.

After all, when you're a kid and you smile at somebody, they smile back.

Other churches started inviting us to sing, because for kids, we were good performers. It's adorable when kids get up and sing, but when those same kids sing *well*, it's pretty amazing.

My father pastored in the Cincinnati area, at the Tylersville Road Church of God. That church was an integral part of my life from age four to fourteen.

Like many families, ours came from a long line of poverty. In those days, ministry jobs didn't pay a living wage and there was an expectation that if you were in ministry, you wouldn't have time for another job. So I have memories of my parents working hard to keep everything afloat financially.

Our family was given clothes, food, essentials. We also ate food from my grandparents' farm. But our living conditions weren't the best. My mom said that when I was a baby, she'd find my pacifiers had been chewed up by rats.

When my family first came to Ohio, the pay was low and the parsonage was run-down, so my dad became a bi-vocational pastor. After Dad started working a second job, we were finally able to get a house of our own.

That's when things started to change for our family. We suddenly began shopping and eating out more often. I specifically remember that Christmas in our home changed at that point too. For one thing, our living room was filled with toys. My mom had always tried to make Christmas nice for us in the past, but our family just didn't have the money.

I was in the fifth grade when my mother decided to get a "real" job. She became a server at Denny's and worked the third shift. During the day Mom was busy babysitting, and at night she waited tables. We woke up each morning to find stacks of dollar bills from her tips. She used her tip money to take us out to lunch on Sundays. Eventually she went back to school at Miami University in Oxford, Ohio. While I was in school, she was earning her nursing degree.

I started doing poorly in school around the third grade. My mom was concerned, but my dad was never really bothered by it. I eventually failed the eighth grade and had to repeat it, so I ended up graduating from high school at age 19. I've thought about it more since then and concluded that I probably just didn't care. School wasn't important. After all, I was going to be a musician. I wasn't learning about music in science class. I wasn't learning about music in math class. Despite what everybody tells you, math and music don't have much to do with each other. If you can count to eight, you can do music. It was the only thing I cared about.

I essentially earned all of my friends through singing. Nearly all my relationships were built around music. We had a pretty large middle school in Fairfield, Ohio—over 1,000 students—and I was the kid who got his shoelaces tied together under his desk. That is, until the day of the school choir concert when I sang my first solo. Suddenly, I felt like the big man on campus. It happened virtually overnight. One day I was completely unknown, the guy everybody picked on if they even acknowledged him, and the next day I was Mr. Popularity, getting a lot of attention—even from the popular girls—because of my voice.

By the early 1990s, singing was a central part of who I was, and I worked hard at it. Those were the days of artists like Whitney Houston, Mariah Carey, and Boyz II Men. They taught my generation a masterclass on jazz scales and vocal dynamics. I spent hours and hours listening to their music on my cassette Walkman. I would hear some crazy vocal line and then stop, rewind, and play it over until I had figured it out note for note. I can still remember every song from those old albums. My hard work paid off: As a somewhat socially awkward kid, I needed a bridge to help me connect with my peers. Singing was that bridge.

While school was a mixed bag for me, our church set me up for success from a spiritual perspective. That church was full of people who poured into me. Buddy and Shirley George were a couple who spoiled us kids. They took us to Cincinnati Reds games and just loved on us. There were other influential people, including youth pastors Rick and Faye Sims and music leader Eddie Hyatt. Keep in mind that this was basically a country church: I played drums, my dad was on the piano, my brother played the organ, and a guy named Brother Gibson was on bass. Eddie was leading *worship*, and I'd never seen it done that way before. Instead of saying, "Turn to page 125," Eddie would say, "We're singing 'All Hail King Jesus.'"

It was great seeing how plugged in my parents were. My dad was a natural leader, and people loved him. I still get emails from people who were at that church telling me how much they miss my dad and our family. The church had about two hundred members, and our youth group was probably thirty-five of those people. It was a great time for building relationships, and many of those kids are still my friends today.

I failed the eighth grade because I was expelled. I got in a fight and a knife fell out of my pocket, since someone had bought me a knife for my birthday. I have no idea what the fight was about or who it was with. I just remember that I was called in to the principal's office, and he expelled me. The incident took place in February or March, so from March to May I stayed home, wasted time, and watched *Days of Our Lives*.

My mother was finishing her nursing degree at the time. She doesn't remember me being expelled. We've talked about it in the last few years, and she says, "No, you weren't. You weren't expelled."

"Yeah, I was," I tell her. "I didn't go to school." I have that memory clearly. She doesn't, but she was busy with classes, and Dad was working a second job. They never spoke to me about my grades. It was simply understood that I failed and I needed to repeat eighth grade. It wasn't a big deal. It was life.

At least I wouldn't be attending the same school. Late that summer, our family moved from Ohio to Wichita, Kansas. It was a time of transition for us. My brother, Keith, was going through some spiritual struggles, and my parents were feeling unsettled. My sister, Rebecca, was doing pretty well, but Mom had just graduated from nursing school and was looking for her first job, so my father told the denomination that he was ready for a change. It turned out that Rolling Hills Church of God in Wichita had an opening for a pastor.

I graduated from high school in Wichita. I became a mediocre disciple of Jesus in Wichita. Our family still gathered together to read the Bible in Wichita, but not quite as much as we did in Ohio. It's interesting that I never considered that detail until now. That's because our lives took strange turns in that city.

It wasn't long before my brother graduated from high school, so he wasn't really plugged into the community. At this point, Keith was the piano guy, and I was the singer. My sister didn't think she had an identity anymore, even though she was probably a better singer than me at the time. People just noticed me more, I guess. As it turned out, Rebecca ended up thriving in the school drama community, and I eventually followed in her footsteps.

But all that took a while. Like I said, our lives took strange turns after that move. After we arrived there, I decided to never do music again.

CHAPTER 3

VILLAGE INN

ALL THREE OF US KIDS were bitter about the move. None of us wanted to leave Ohio. We left behind friends, family members, and teachers who had helped and encouraged us. My brother had a serious girlfriend at the time. That relationship fell apart, as well as the rock band he was part of. The move was traumatic.

Meanwhile, my voice was changing, and suddenly I couldn't sing as well. My voice cracked and my vocal range shriveled. Given the nature of my early teenage awkwardness, the last thing I wanted to do was embarrass myself by singing in front of people.

My performing days were over—at least that's what I

decided. My parents, however, had different plans. They encouraged me to keep practicing and reassured me that I was just going through a temporary slump.

After our family relocated to Wichita, my father wanted his kids to perform "Peace Speaker," a song we'd sung countless times before. It was Dad's first Sunday as the new pastor, and it took all the courage I could muster to stand in front of the congregation. I sang the alto part, and the notes that used to wow audiences in my younger days were too high for me. My voice cracked several times; I was mortified. There was polite applause when we finished, but I noticed that not everyone was clapping.

After the service, one of the older men from the congregation made his way to me. "Thanks for singing for us this morning," he said with a smile. "That song seemed way too high. I was worried about you for a minute there!" I'm sure he was just trying to help, but my heart was crushed. It was the first negative thing anyone had ever said to me about my singing.

I didn't tell anyone about that conversation, and my father eventually asked me to sing in church again. This time I chose a number that was a little easier on my eighth-grade vocal range. Modest applause again, with one exception. Sure enough, that same man found his way over to me after the service. This time, it was to tell me that I'd sung off-key— more specifically, my pitch was flat—before he encouraged me to find better breath support exercises.

We were a family of singers, and when we performed in

Ohio, people went nuts. When we came to Wichita . . . no reaction. Nobody seemed to care if I could sing, and to make matters worse, I felt criticized any time I had to sing. I was sick of it, and I didn't want to perform in public anymore. For a while after that, my parents could only convince me to sing in church if I was part of a group.

My parents don't know this, but I barely went to class in the eighth grade. I spent my days painting murals all over the walls and painting sets for the school plays, while my teachers just gave me passing grades. I did attend French class because I had to learn a foreign language, but I spent many periods outside the classroom with a paintbrush in hand. I provided free labor for the school, and they entered my art in several competitions. One of my paintings won a statewide prize, and it hung for a while in the capitol building. That's when I decided to be an artist.

I was thriving at art, but I still didn't have many friends. Those friends I'd earned before? They were all back in Ohio. I was beginning to form tight relationships with other young people at the church, but I didn't really know anyone at school.

The next year I finally moved on to Northwest High School, where you had to choose your one favorite creative program. You couldn't be in band *and* choir. You couldn't do art *and* anything else. All these classes took place during the same hour, so I chose art over music.

Coincidentally, that's also when I started smoking pot. It was symptomatic of just how much my life had shifted since the move. I had been part of the "Just Say No to Drugs" club in Ohio, yet by my freshman year in Wichita, I was smoking weed. Back then I had a record by Cypress Hill, a band that supported marijuana use. The album art included a rationale explaining why weed was a gift from God. At first I thought, "This is ridiculous!" After I read it again, I became completely convinced by their argument. After all, I reasoned, every other substance people take has additives. Moreover, pot grows on a plant that God made. I somehow persuaded myself that smoking weed was a spiritual thing to do.

Even in high school I was completely comfortable as a loner. I was an introvert, and I was someone who'd learned to communicate through music to the point that I had difficulty communicating without it.

Everything changed at our high school talent show when my sister asked me to sing a duet. We always sang duets when we were younger. But Rebecca's confidence had been shaken in high school, and she didn't want to go onstage by herself. The director scheduled us to open the event. We sang "A Whole New World," and it just blew up. We did great, and the audience cheered.

Once again it was a turning point. I landed a part in a school play along with Rebecca. I was a freshman, my sister was a senior, and I had a whole new crowd of friends made up of all these drama people. Everybody knew who I was after that talent show. I was invited to join the choir. It was amazing to see the effect that singing had on my social life.

It restored a bit of my confidence, so I agreed to start

singing in church again. As the years passed, I kept improving and became serious again about music as a profession. Yet as far as I can remember, I never sang a solo in my father's church when that "old man" didn't make some comment about my performance. Even though I dreaded it, I endured it so I could continue to grow as a singer. From time to time I even took his advice.

Keep in mind that I would one day perform in front of millions on *American Idol* for perhaps the most infamous critical bully in show business. Not only did I face Simon Cowell each week, the internet was full of critics who bashed both me and my fellow contestants from one end to the next. Every week some of the nation's most popular publications described how poorly we'd performed.

If that mean old man hadn't toughened my skin, I might not have been emotionally prepared for *Idol*. Thanks to his persistent feedback, I learned to embrace the naysayers and critics. I attempted to learn from those who meant well and ignore those who didn't. Whether I realized it or not, I was ready for Simon Cowell.

After my stint on *American Idol*, that same man from church came to one of my Wichita concerts. He found me backstage after the show, tearfully embraced me, and told me how incredibly proud he was to know me. I did a great job, he said. It was a powerful moment, and I felt nothing but gratitude. It changed my whole memory of him and unveiled the massive support I had from that church without even realizing it. I recognized something that day: Even when I thought he was just a mean old man—even if he *was* a mean old man—God had used this person to prepare me for His purpose (Romans 8:28).

Most of my buddies in Wichita worked at the local Village Inn restaurant, so I got a job there. Seeing these other guys with an extra $100 a week to spend made me say, "I want that too!"

It didn't take long to realize I wasn't a good server. For some reason, I couldn't do it. I took too long getting drinks, fumbled food trays, forgot simple things like dropping off checks. It was all one big struggle. My difficulties eventually gave me a complex: I couldn't understand why I had so much trouble with tasks that came easily for others. Maybe something was seriously wrong with me. Since I was also struggling in school at the time, I thought that perhaps I was fundamentally flawed, dumb, and just not up to par.

Village Inn trained me to be a server, but most nights I worked as a busboy because I couldn't catch on. I couldn't even greet customers properly when they came in. I was actually terrified to greet people—I was afraid of people in general.

(You might wonder how I was ever able to get onstage and perform in front of an audience, and I'm not sure how to explain it. I was comfortable onstage, always have been. But get me offstage, and I was terrified.)

My manager believed that in time I'd be able to overcome my many shortcomings, but after several weeks on the job, I wasn't improving. Instead of firing me, he'd give me a section with just one table so I could get used to handling orders one at a time. My manager also learned never to schedule me as a server on busy nights. At least on Monday and Tuesday nights I could say I was a server even though they tried to avoid seating anybody in my section.

Yet it was on that exact sort of night when I learned a truly life-changing lesson.

━━━━━━

It was a couple of months into my Village Inn job on a Monday evening that was even slower than most. The entire staff was sitting around doing nothing, just twiddling our thumbs. Back then—this was the mid-1990s—the restaurant was divided into two sections: smoking on the left and non-smoking on the right. We all sat at a round table in the smoking section.

Soon everyone was complaining about how we never made any serious money. In fact, we said, we should all just quit. Somebody had the bright idea that it would be funny to quit that night because the manager was already gone; he'd given us the keys as he left.

"Guys, the place is empty," he said. "Just lock up when you're done." It was the first time he'd ever done that, so the staff thought it was the perfect night to pull a prank. I don't know why we thought it would be funny to leave the place empty, but for some reason we did.

Still, I knew instinctively that it was a disrespectful thing to do. So I stayed and watched as, one by one, all my buddies left. They walked to their cars and drove away. We began the evening with about ten staffers in the restaurant; before long only three of us remained.

Everyone walked out except for Paul, a cook; Jennifer, a host; and me. I was the only person left on the serving and bus staff. The three of us just sat there, watching the time tick away. Soon enough it was 9:00 p.m., which meant we had only an hour until closing time.

That's when the cars started showing up. The three of us watched in horror and amazement as the parking lot quickly filled, like a big concert was about to start. We had no idea where all these people were coming from. It turns out there was an Amway convention in Wichita that night, and no one at the restaurant knew about it. What's more, the convention was right down the road, so afterward they all headed to the nearest Village Inn. What did these folks want? Pie and coffee and a place to talk about Amway for the next few hours. Who offers those things in abundance? Village Inn.

The customers started walking in, and Jennifer immediately started seating people. Paul started working too, and he was solid. But me? I was completely incompetent. At that point I'd never served more than one table at a time. Jennifer and Paul went about their business, but I was thinking, *I can't do this*. I was terrified. I was sweating.

I had a quick flash of regret. *Why hadn't I left when my friends did?* I knew why. I wasn't authorized to make those kinds of decisions. I didn't belong to myself. No, I belonged to a father, and my father would not be okay if I bailed on my job.

My parents had instilled in me a sense of honor, so I knew that walking out was wrong. On the other hand, I knew I wasn't a good server, and I wasn't making much money because they only paid me to bus tables. Servers made more than busboys, so they were getting a heck of a deal with me. *I shouldn't even work here anymore,* I thought. *I should just quit.*

In desperation I called my dad from the pay phone. "Dad," I began. "I'm in a very difficult situation. I need you to get me out of this. It's too much. I'm not strong enough. I can't do it. I know that if you just say the word, I won't have to go through it. Please, don't make do this."

There was a pause before my father spoke. "Well, Son, do you want to be a boy, or do you want to be a man?"

Unfortunately, I had absolutely no interest in being a man at that moment. "I don't know," I replied. "What do you want me to do? You always said that I'm your special little boy!"

I was trying to talk my way out of it, and again there was a pause while my dad considered his words.

Even at age sixteen, I knew there was no one on earth who rooted for me like my father. He saw the moment as an opportunity for me to learn something invaluable. If I quit, he would still love me. He probably would have met me at the front door with a hug, maybe even a Bible verse encouraging me to press forward.

"What do you want me to do?" I asked.

"I want you to do what you've committed yourself to do."

He was teaching me how to be a man. And because of what I knew about him—how much he loved me, wanted the best for me, had high hopes for me—I submitted my will to my father's. Instead of trusting my own instincts, I trusted his.

He helped me calm down; he took some of the pressure off. At that point I wasn't even doing it for Village Inn anymore; I was doing it for my dad. Because my dad is a man of honor, it didn't matter if I got fired from my job after that night. Simply by staying I would make my dad proud.

By the time I hung up the phone, the entire restaurant was packed. Every table was occupied. I jumped up on the host station and greeted everyone at once.

"Excuse me, everyone!" I began. "May I have your attention? Welcome to Village Inn!"

Some people cheered.

"The bad news," I continued, "is that I'm your only server, and I'm not very good. But if you'll be patient with me, I'll take care of you to the best of my ability! Does that sound okay?" More cheering followed, and a small group in one corner began chanting: "Amway, Amway, Amway." At least the crowd seemed forgiving. For now.

I began to strategize how to navigate this chaos. We had some paper children's menus, the kind with no writing on the back so kids could color on them. I grabbed one and began sketching a basic layout of the restaurant, trying to science my way to good serving.

After a couple of minutes, I felt I had finally cracked the code . . . to serving two, maybe even three tables at once. But what good did that do me? I was staring at a completely full restaurant! This task wasn't just too much for *me*, it was too much for *anyone*. I could have been the greatest server in history and I still couldn't handle this job. There were too many tables, too many customers. It was only a matter of time before people would begin complaining. Soon, I imagined, an entire restaurant full of people would walk out—and it would be my fault. A rush of emotions hit me like a wrecking ball: I had listened to my dad, but he was wrong.

In that moment my whole attitude switched—from *I can do this* to *There's no way I can do this*. In a heartbeat I went from feeling so much love for my dad to feeling completely alone. *Why wouldn't he let me quit?* The transition happened so quickly that by the time I got to the first table I was already defeated.

Jennifer wasn't helping. You'd think she'd start going around the room collecting drink orders, but she was busy waiting for more people to come in. There wasn't a single seat available in the entire restaurant, and she just stood at the host's station. I'd been abandoned.

While I was taking that first table's drink requests, I looked down at my notepad and wondered, *Do I even have enough paper for this?* I looked up and saw people in booths and tables all around. They seemed to be getting antsy, periodically glancing in my direction. I noticed a small crowd still gathered at the front of the restaurant. Every time the door opened a little bell chimed, signaling still more customers coming in. I was losing it.

That's when it happened. The little bell chimed again and I turned toward it. I did a double take. *Could it really be?* Sure enough, standing right there at the front door was my father. *What's he doing here?*

Dad walked up and said, "Son, how can I help you?"

The same man who I thought had forsaken me actually knew just how much I needed him. Instead of "teaching me a lesson," he showed up to help.

I handed him the paper in my hand. "Can you get these drinks for me?"

"Yeah," he said.

His presence showed me that I wasn't alone. He worked alongside me for the rest of the night, serving drinks, rolling silverware, whatever we needed. Jennifer started helping deliver orders to the tables, or at least helping me tray the orders. Dad was also traying orders, at least when he wasn't busy making salads. He had no idea what ingredients went in them—he might have used the photos on the menu for guidance. Most of all, he stayed with me.

It took three or four hours before all the customers finally left. The cook was frustrated, throwing dishes against the wall because of all the food orders. You'd think these folks would just want pie and coffee, but they ordered pancakes and skillets and all this stuff, and he was in the kitchen all alone.

The place was trashed. It was filthy. There were no bussers to help clear the tables, so you can imagine what the place looked like after the crowd left. We didn't finish cleaning up until three o'clock in the morning.

I will never forget how my heart leapt when my dad appeared, like a guardian angel telling me, "Don't worry. I've got you." Don't get me wrong—the evening was still stressful; there was still so much to do. But with my father beside me, I knew everything was going to be okay. And it was.

It was an award-winning moment for my dad. More than anything, he reflected our heavenly Father to me. In fact, in the midst of the mayhem, I reflected on Scriptures from my childhood that suddenly came alive to me, including "God is our refuge and strength, a very present help in trouble" (Psalm 46:1) and "Be strong and courageous. Do not fear or be in dread of them, for it is the LORD your God who goes with you. He will not leave you or forsake you" (Deuteronomy 31:6).

That night was like a Bible lesson, not just because of those Scriptures, but because I saw God through my earthly father. My dad is a good man, but that moment was special; it was different. I matured that night. Because I obeyed him, I grew.

What's more, the customers we served that night were incredibly generous with their tips. More importantly, I received a crash course on serving multiple tables. I learned how to connect with customers even when the place was busy. For two months I had been a disgrace to the restaurant industry, and in one night I became a capable server.

One evening changed my whole life. Until that moment, I thought I was bad at serving for the same reason I didn't do well at school: I couldn't grasp serving because I was dumb; I couldn't grasp school because I was dumb. I had accepted that perception as fact, until I learned in just one night how to serve an entire restaurant full of people. And within a couple of weeks I was training the new servers—replacements for all my buddies who left that night.

───

It's difficult to convey how much I grew up in just one night. My attitude and work habits improved, both at the restaurant and in school. I loved my youth group, and I loved listening to my dad's sermons.

And I still loved smoking weed.

If I'm honest, I have to admit that weed ended up impacting me in other areas. Marijuana makes you feel as if nothing else matters. I had no problem, for example, with skipping classes. I got high almost every day. I got high at lunchtime, on my way home from school, on my way to work. I think some people knew, but no one talked about it. Not a single person asked me about it. My dad was a part-time drug counselor. I had bloodshot eyes and reeked of weed, and yet he never raised the issue.

I gave up on visual art and started singing again. But not in church, not if I could help it. I felt that some church people made fun of me, but at school they loved me. So that was my fulfillment—getting high, singing in my high school choir, and working at Village Inn.

Ironically, serving tables now made me feel good about myself. All because I'd obeyed my father. That experience helped prepare me for hardships I would face later on in life. Indeed, hardships are inevitable, and I was about to face the scariest moment of my life.

CHAPTER 4

DIVINE PROTECTION

MY MOTHER NEVER, ever interrupted my father when he was preaching. Not at any time. Not for any reason. It just wasn't done. So I can't imagine the congregation's reaction that night when she rose to her feet in the middle of my dad's sermon.

Mom had tears in her eyes and was visibly shaking. She asked for everyone's attention. She asked if they could pause and pray for me. She asked if they could do it right now.

"I feel like he's in danger."

At least, that's the way I heard it happened. I can't say for sure, because I wasn't there. But I wasn't far. At that moment, I was just a couple hundred feet away—standing in a driveway on the other side of the church parking lot with the barrel of a gun pressed against my head.

What is divine protection? For one thing, it's something plenty of us desire. Many of the prayer requests I hear these days are from people seeking assurance for a loved one or for themselves—that they'll be protected from danger or misfortune. But I've also read the stories of Peter, Paul, Stephen, and other early church leaders who were martyred because of their faith. Then there's Moses, who spent forty years wandering in the wilderness and died without ever experiencing the Promised Land. There's Daniel, who was hauled away into Babylonian exile along with so many others. There's even the great King David, who spent a large part of his life running from those who wished to kill him. In fact, I don't know of one major player in the Bible who was completely spared from harm, who didn't face hardship in one way or another.

Does this mean there's no such thing as divine protection? Of course not. Scripture reminds us again and again that the mighty hand of God was guiding each one of these men. That His watchful eye was always present. That He was, in fact, working things together for their good.

But as a teenager, I wasn't overly concerned with my protection—divine or otherwise. I was just glad I didn't get hurt when I foolishly decided to test the maneuverability of my used Mazda convertible by speeding around the neighborhood. Instead of demonstrating my driving prowess, I ended up hitting a neighbor's curb.

By the fall of 1995, I was a high school sophomore, my mother was a nurse, and my dad was pastor of Rolling Hills Church of God. At school I was a skinny theater kid who worked most nights at the nearby Village Inn. When I wasn't at school or work, I could often be found at church.

I didn't love everything about my teen years, but I still loved going to church. We had a tight-knit youth group, everyone got along, and there weren't any cliques. Most of the youth were children of committed church members. I'll admit that I probably enjoyed church more as a social function than an opportunity to pursue Jesus. Maybe that's because our house was already in a constant state of "church service." The parsonage where we lived was right next to the church building, my dad was the pastor, and my mom taught Sunday school. My family used to spend hours singing, praying, or just talking about God.

But now both Keith and Rebecca were away at Lee University in Cleveland, Tennessee, which left my parents and me in the house. This made for a peaceful (and somewhat boring) home life. My classmates were great, but they weren't exactly committed Christians. My church friends understood me better. Any time the church was open, most of them were there too.

My schedule at Village Inn kept me from attending some of the evening services. That was the case one Sunday night in December, when I didn't arrive back home until well after dark. Because my car was in the shop following my encounter with the curb, I was using my mother's. It was a Saturn sedan, forest green and virtually brand new. My mom had worked as a nurse for nearly four years before she finally saved enough to buy a new car.

As I drove home, I considered whether or not I could still slip into the service without causing too much distraction. By the time I rolled into the driveway, I'd already decided to stay home rather than walk in late.

Back then we had a manual garage door, so I left the car running while I stepped out of the car. That's when I heard heavy footsteps rapidly approaching from behind.

The man looked ominous. He was solidly built with a large frame. If I recall correctly, he was dressed mostly in black and wore a dark baseball cap. His face was covered, bandit style, but I could see his eyes. I will never forget his eyes: They were dark, and they were angry.

At first I thought he was just looking for a fight. He approached me with an aggressive posture, but with his mouth covered I couldn't quite make out what he was saying. I didn't want any trouble, so I politely asked, "Can I help you?"

His right hand raised, and that's when I saw the gun.

His voice grew louder. "I said, step away from the ___ car!"

I instantly recognized what an easy target I was. I'd left a brand-new sedan running in the driveway. If this guy was looking to steal a car, I'd practically gift wrapped it for him. I knew this was a dangerous situation, but I also didn't want to lose Mom's car! I started to resist.

Any fight I had in me evaporated the moment he shoved

me up against the garage door. I promptly resolved to cooperate fully. He held me back with one arm, yelling and cursing and waving the gun in my face. He was very angry, and I was very afraid, but I figured he just wanted the car. I would gladly give it to him.

Finally, just when I thought he was about to take the car and leave, he instead cocked his gun and placed the cold steel against my forehead. At that moment a feeling of finality overcame me. It's difficult to explain, but I was convinced my life was finished. I knew he was there to kill me.

———

One thing you notice when tragedy strikes is that you instantly embrace the power of prayer as never before. It doesn't matter if you've followed the Lord for ninety years or if you've never been to church a day in your life. Even the most outspoken atheists can experience a change of heart when life gets desperate. I've received their messages on Facebook: "Phil, do you mind sending up a prayer for my wife?"

It's natural to pray with a gun pressed against your head, but I didn't bother asking for protection. I guess it was because I felt that death was imminent. Instead I prayed that God would give me the strength to die bravely. I asked God to forgive my sins. I asked Him to bring peace to my parents and siblings and to bring me home to Him. I closed my eyes and waited for the gunshot, perhaps the last sound I'd ever hear.

I imagined the horror on my poor mother's face when she walked home to find her son lying in the driveway with a bullet hole in his head. I thought about my brother and sister away at school; how would they hear about it? I thought about my sweet father and what this would do to him. I thought about my friends, my funeral, even the proclamation of my death over the loudspeaker at school during morning announcements. I thought about how all my dreams were about to die with me.

All these thoughts flashed by in seconds, but in my mind it lasted an eternity.

It was long enough that I started to wonder if this guy was ever going to get on with it! I sensed the metal leave my forehead, but I didn't hear him back away. I figured he was simply putting some space between the barrel and me for a cleaner shot. Yet he paused. And paused. And still nothing. I slowly opened one eye to see if he'd left, but he was still standing there, right in front of me.

But now he was shaking nervously and was looking above me, as if reading words over my head—words that only he could see. His eyes, once filled with wrath, had changed. They'd widened. He even looked, dare I say, afraid. He looked in my eyes and his gun shook wildly as he slowly backed away. He backed up until he'd reached the car door. He climbed in and drove away.

It suddenly hit me that he had my key chain. I actually called out, "Hey man, can I get my house key?" as he sped off down the street. You can probably guess how that worked out.

Once again, I knew I would probably distract the congregation if I walked in late during the church service, but I had little choice but to swallow my pride and ask my mom for a house key. I honestly wasn't sure what to do next. Maybe I could use a phone at the church to call 911.

———

I walked into the sanctuary to find everyone up at the altar. Now, this wasn't that unusual for a Pentecostal church like ours. What was unusual was that there was no music, no preaching. There were maybe fifty people at church that night, and all of them were gathered around my mother in prayer.

Someone (I believe it was the music director, known to everyone as Brother Wise) spotted me: "Hey, there he is!" Suddenly everyone was looking at me.

I walked up to Mom and told her that a masked gunman had just stolen her car. She first made sure I was okay, then she and my father went together to the church office to call the police. When they left the sanctuary, people started asking me what happened.

When I recounted the details, they just marveled and smiled. I asked what they were smiling about, and someone said my mother had interrupted Dad's sermon by standing up in tears. As I was saying my final prayers in the driveway, Mom was asking for everyone's attention—if they could all stop and pray because she sensed I was in danger. They quickly gathered at the altar.

Not long after, I walked in to tell them that, in fact, my life *had* been in danger. Everyone was amazed. They believed that Mom had heard from the Holy Spirit and that their prayers had succeeded in saving my life. Probably in a bit of shock, I saw it as nothing more than a strange coincidence, even though I knew my mom had never before interrupted my dad's sermons for any reason.

I headed back to the house with Mom and Dad to wait for the police to arrive. I think Mom was nervous that the car thief might come back to finish the job when he realized he'd left a witness alive.

Several police cars were soon scattered around the church parking lot. I don't remember how many officers showed up, but I do remember that the gentleman who questioned me was wearing FBI identification around his neck. He asked me questions about how I survived the incident. Did I say anything that triggered the gunman? Were there any other witnesses?

I remember wondering why an FBI agent was present. My mom told me I was lucky to be alive, but I was still confused. I asked one of the officers why my mother would say something like that. He told me that if the gunman was who they suspected it might be, then our driveway was just the latest stop on his multi-state crime spree. Furthermore, he wasn't alone.

As it turned out, I was now a witness in a national case. I later learned there were actually two men outside our house that night: the one who held me up at gunpoint and a partner who had left another stolen vehicle right around the corner. Both were armed and dangerous. They had traveled north from Texas, through Oklahoma, and on to Wichita. They had taken multiple vehicles in an attempt to keep the authorities off of their trail. With each car they stole, they left a dead body behind. I was the only victim who survived.

In that moment, when the FBI agent confirmed to me that I could have died—that I should have died—I began to wonder if there really was more going on than I'd first imagined. A picture started forming in my mind. While this man held a gun to my head, my mom interrupted our church service and asked the congregation to pray for my protection. When I opened my eyes in the driveway, the gunman was nervously looking above me, as if he'd seen writing—or perhaps an angel.

What exactly did he see? What, exactly, was protecting me? I'll probably never know, but I do know that something broke inside of him that night. No matter what he saw, I began to realize that God had, in fact, intervened on my behalf—even if it was just to demonstrate that He was my source of protection and that I had nothing to fear.

A few days later, we learned from the police that Mom's car had been located and the two men were in custody. I was eventually called to serve as a witness, but I never had to testify, since both men pled guilty to the charges against them.

———

I believe I experienced divine protection that night. It wasn't simply that I was spared from a traumatic experience; it was that God gave me the grace to continue in the mission He had planned for me.

I also realize that for every story like mine, there's the tragic story of someone who did not survive the encounter. God is sovereign over all things. His view of death is not the same as ours. Sometimes we get caught up in the idea that death is our ultimate loss, but for those who believe in Jesus Christ, death is actually the door that leads to our ultimate reward. I believe there's great rejoicing in heaven when a believer finishes his or her earthly trials. There is no more sickness or loss, trials or temptations. Instead, the departed believer enters into the joy of the Kingdom, forever and ever. My grasp of this fact became so real that, for a time, I wondered why God spared me that night in the driveway.

Why didn't God allow me to end my journey there? I believe it's because He was not finished with me. He had a plan for me—a divine destiny. That plan included college, the Navy, and a family. That plan included *American Idol.* And that plan, ultimately, included allowing me to share my faith in Christ with millions of people all over the world. I also believe that when I've completed my appointed tasks, my time on earth will come to an end.

God has a plan for you, too. Your life is not an accident. There's a sovereign God who has called you and chosen you. You are right where you need to be. He's stationed you in the same way that the U.S. Navy later stationed me in Florida. If you call yourself a Christian, then your purpose is to share the gospel and make disciples. If the love of God has been revealed to you, it's so you can reflect that same love to the people around you.

The Bible is filled with testimonies forged in the midst of trials. The apostle Paul was bitten by a deadly viper and simply shook it off. Moses crossed the Red Sea on dry ground. Peter walked on water. Daniel survived a night in a den of hungry lions. David defeated the great warrior Goliath. In each case, it wasn't by their own strength or by their own hand that they accomplished these things. It was by the mighty hand of God.

Just as we see adversity throughout the Scriptures, we also see divine protection.

Jesus encouraged us to seek first the Kingdom of God and His righteousness because He knew that we're easily distracted. We're quick to shift our focus from others to ourselves, and when we see only our own needs, we have a tendency to fear. We worry about our health, our finances, our children. But when we believe in Jesus, we begin to trust Him too. We trust that our health is in His hands, that He will supply all of our needs, that He is sovereign even over our families.

When I was a child, I knew my parents would take care of me. When we rode in the car, I knew my father's hands were on the wheel. If I can trust my earthly parents, how much more can I trust the One who spoke everything into existence? As Paul said in Romans 8:38-39, "For I am sure that neither death nor life, nor angels nor rulers, nor things present nor things to come, nor powers, nor height nor depth, nor anything else in all creation, will be able to separate us from the love of God in Christ Jesus our Lord."

That sounds a lot like divine protection to me.

CHAPTER 5

MOVING OUT

———

I ABSOLUTELY BELIEVE that God Himself spared me that night in the driveway. So what did I do the very next day?

I bought a gun.

I approached a friend at school who was connected to people of, well, ill repute, and I asked how I could buy a gun. It cost about $100, and of course it was purchased illegally.

Let me make this clear: God had just protected me in much the same way that He took the children of Israel through the Red Sea. Yet those same people still did stupid stuff. I think it's important to acknowledge that I am also a child of Israel. I'm that guy who walked through the parted Red Sea and then complained to Moses about how I'm going to die in the wilderness.

I kept the gun in my bedroom. I took it to school with me, but I didn't take it inside. I left it in my car, usually in the glove compartment. By then my Mazda convertible was repaired, and I felt super cool again.

After a few weeks I felt weird about owning a loaded gun, so I eventually gave it back to my friend. I don't know if he ever returned it to the person who sold it to me.

I'll admit that this was a strange season of life. I was in love with Jesus and spending time in personal devotions every day. I was praying every day. I look back and think, *Man, I was in love with Jesus—and I was still smoking weed!*

At this point I started to recognize that I was still just a child in the faith. I needed to be more mature. Whether I was in ministry someday or not, I was still a disciple of Jesus. I had an intimate relationship with God, yet I also enjoyed getting high. The dichotomy began to weigh on me. *I shouldn't be doing this. It's affecting me in other areas.* So I decided that I wasn't going to stay in Wichita. I was originally planning to attend Wichita State University, but I concluded that maybe I wouldn't go to college at all. I asked my parents for permission to quit high school, but they wouldn't let me. "I'm going to be a musician," I argued, but my parents insisted that I graduate.

I had great friends in Wichita, but spiritually speaking it wasn't a great place for me to be. It was time for me to move forward. The moment I graduated, I drove to Cleveland, Tennessee, to be with my older brother, Keith.

Cleveland seemed like a spiritual oasis. There are more than a hundred churches within the city limits as well as the headquarters of the denomination in which I was raised. My brother had returned to Lee University after a year away, so I just moved in with him. Keith had a job and was already dating the girl who would become my sister-in-law, so I didn't see either of them much. I didn't know anyone else in Cleveland, and I spent most of that first summer friendless.

I wasn't planning to attend college when I arrived in Cleveland in the summer of 1997, but I'd always admired the Lee University Singers. The Lee Singers, as they are better known, are a prestigious touring group of about sixty students who excel vocally. They are amazing to see in concert. My father had been a member several decades before, and both Keith and Rebecca spent time touring with them. When I saw the audition posters around campus, I decided to try out.

I hadn't even enrolled in classes when Keith accompanied me for my audition. The audition panel alone was intimidating, with the group's director, Dr. Walt Mauldin—a man I had admired for more than a decade—front and center. I felt good about my performance, but better singers than me had been passed on before. I tried to keep my expectations in check, but that didn't prevent me from racing to the music building when the results were posted. I was thrilled to see my name on the list. (Rebecca didn't make it in the Lee Singers until her second semester, although her voice topped mine. But apparently guys who could sing were in short supply.)

My original plan was to take some time off from school and put more thought into what I wanted to do with my life. I knew college was a tremendous expense and a substantial commitment, and I didn't want to major in music just because I couldn't think of anything else. Joining the Lee Singers forced my hand. I might have been the last person to register for classes, but I was thrilled to be a member of the legendary group.

At Lee University, a musical group is like a fraternity or sorority. We spent nearly every weekend together as well as four hours each week in rehearsals. We traveled together and played countless pranks on one another. Yet by the end of the first semester, I still hadn't made any close friends, since my introverted nature made developing friendships difficult. Back then I was a lonesome young man in the midst of a crowd.

⸻

During the week my emphasis was school; on the weekends it was the group. The Lee Singers was a big deal for me, and the experience was all-encompassing. The group was the best training I've had, hands down. We performed in churches, auditoriums, and concert halls.

At one point in the middle of the first semester, my brother and I realized we didn't have any money. I wasn't working because I was traveling with the Lee Singers, and Keith wasn't working because he was also traveling as the accompanist for the Ladies of Lee, the university's all-female choir. Neither of us had scholarships, and my parents were already helping us cover basic bills like a car and rent. Apparently we hadn't considered the cost of food, and now we were starving.

As long as Keith was dating his girlfriend, we could always raid her cabinets. But they had broken up for a time, so that was currently not an option. We had survived extended periods without eating before, but after about three days I remember being concerned. It's one thing to not eat because you don't feel hungry, but when you're skipping meals because you have to, you worry.

We thought about asking our parents for help, but they were already struggling to maintain their current level of support. I did get a restaurant job; however, I was still two weeks away from my first paycheck.

Keith and I started praying for God to provide food. We believed that God works miracles, so we figured He could certainly feed us. One day we woke up feeling compelled to go to the grocery store because God had a plan. God prompted us to go, and we did. We did something that made no sense on a human level.

We climbed into my car, which was almost out of gas because we didn't have money for gas either, and I started driving. We didn't even notice the nearby Walmart because we were so busy talking.

"What if God wants to buy our groceries for us? We've

been buying ramen noodles all semester—what are we going to eat if God's footing the bill? We can get anything we want!" We discussed all of our favorite foods, which is apparently what you talk about when you're starving.

Keith and I lived on one side of Cleveland, and the school was on the other side of town. We ended up driving right by Walmart but stopped at a little grocery store near the university called Watson's. As we walked up and down the aisles, we tossed everything we wanted into the grocery cart. Everything! We grabbed ground beef, chicken, Hamburger Helper, Fruity Pebbles cereal—all the good stuff—and when it was rung up, the bill was over $300. I was embarrassed watching the clerk scan these groceries because I knew I didn't have a dollar in my pocket.

That's when our Aunt Myra walked into the store. Aunt Myra lived in Crossville, Tennessee, which is about ninety minutes north of Cleveland. We had no idea she was even in town that day. It turns out she was visiting a friend and needed some groceries. For some reason, same as we did, Aunt Myra drove right by the big Walmart. She ended up, same as we did, on the other side of town at that little Watson's grocery store—just as the clerk was about to announce our bill.

The first thing Aunt Myra said was, "I'm so glad I ran into you boys. I wanted to buy some groceries for you."

As far as we were concerned, Aunt Myra was like an angel of the Lord that day.

When Aunt Myra died a couple of years ago, we made a video about the grocery store incident and how much it affected us. The experience taught me that God provides; I'm not providing for myself. Worrying about how *I* was going to provide didn't help, but when I relied on God, He handled it.

When you join the Lee Singers, you sign a "community covenant," a pledge to abstain from worldly behavior including drinking, smoking, and partying. *Okay,* I thought, *I can do that.* But by my second semester, I was guilty of all of the above.

One of the reasons I'd moved to Cleveland was to surround myself with super-Christians, but that wasn't the crowd I fell in with. Much like me, my first real friend at college was in a weird, spiritually dark place. He hung out with others who were just as self-destructive, and I followed him into that group.

As 1997 turned into 1998, I'd somehow managed to find the same sort of crowd I'd hung with in Wichita. They were pot smokers too, and it wasn't long before I quit school. I didn't actually drop out—I just stopped attending classes, including rehearsals. I considered myself out of the Lee Singers because of the covenant. No one in the group knew I was smoking weed, but I was an honorable person. I couldn't be part of it and smoke weed too, and I enjoyed smoking weed more than performing. My life was in a downward spiral.

During that second semester, my new friend and I, along with another guy, spent most of our time with a group of three girls. There wasn't anything romantic happening; we were just buddies. We were all in Cleveland for the same reason, but we all found the same emptiness. And empty people feeling empty together can be a dangerous thing.

The other guys liked to sing too, and I have to admit that we sounded good. We sang some gospel music, and somehow my dad heard about us and invited us to sing at his church in Wichita. When we drove there to do the concert, a couple of the girls from our gang came along.

They took an offering for us at the church that night, and as we headed home, we stopped to get gas. While I was filling up the van, the rest of them spent every last dollar of that church offering on liquor. It was awful; they were completely wasted. I remember being extremely convicted. *We just took God's money. We took the widow's mite and spent it on liquor, and now they are wasted.*

We stopped for the night in St. Louis that Saturday, so the next morning we went to church. That Sunday I had a dramatic encounter with God. His question to me was clear: *Which is more important to you? Having friends or having Me? Because you're going to have to make a choice. You can't have both right now; that's not the way it is.*

It was actually my second encounter in as many days. Before we left on the Wichita trip we had all been hanging out at the girls' apartment. I was smoking a joint outside in the snow when I suddenly felt God's presence telling me, "I don't want you to do that. I don't want you smoking weed."

I put out the joint, and I never smoked pot again. Simple as that.

I'd already made one decision; now it was time for another. For the first time in a long time I had a group of friends, but God was telling me to make a choice. Who did I want more—Him or my buddies?

When we got back to Cleveland, I asked my friends to sit down in a circle. It was the most awkward thing ever.

"Guys," I said, "I feel like I have to choose between my relationship with God and my relationship with you, and I can't choose you; that would be dumb of me."

Surprisingly, they were all cool with it. "Yeah," they said. "We get it." In fact, it was like that moment jump-started a period of self-reflection among the entire group. My first friend from that time is in ministry today, and all of the girls ended up as missionaries or ministry leaders.

I might have been without friends again, but I was close to God and I was completely comfortable with just me and Him.

Life is a series of choices. Each choice we make has the power to alter our lives forever. I knew the choices I'd been making were toxic, but I didn't yet understand just how powerful one positive choice could be.

I would soon find out.

In the summer of 1998 I traveled to China with the Lee Singers, and that's where I had one of the most powerful encounters of my life. I was in the second story of a building where Christians were praying, and the building started shaking—*physically shaking*. I naturally thought we were in the midst of an earthquake.

"No," one of the Chinese Christians told me. "When we pray the building shakes."

"That's ridiculous," I said. "That doesn't make any sense."

And yet, every time they started praying, the building began to shake. It reminded me of Acts 4:31, "And when they had prayed, the place in which they were gathered together was shaken, and they were all filled with the Holy Spirit and continued to speak the word of God with boldness."

It was unbelievable. I discovered that many things in China are different; Christians there are persecuted for their faith, they're imprisoned for their beliefs. There's also a tremendous difference between the relationship Chinese Christians have with God and what most of us have here in America. In America we attend church. We're part of a club. In China, a Christian's faith is a matter of life and death. There's a sense that God has chosen them to spread His glorious gospel throughout a communist nation. The believers in China feel an urgent responsibility to be dedicated, to be legit.

Inside the Buddhist temples, I watched people cry and bow in front of statues. We visited pagodas, and it was jarring to see people burning incense and falling on their faces. I'd never witnessed such fervent worship. It made me realize that I'd never worshiped God like that, that intensely, yet these people were bowing down to *idols*. That experience led me to pray, "I want to worship You, God, in spirit and in truth."

One day a couple of us Lee Singers came across a karaoke setup in a public square. We thought it would be bold to use the microphone to start preaching the gospel, so first we sang, and then we started talking about Jesus. I don't think anybody understood a word we said, but some police officers started getting uneasy, so we left.

On that same trip, I helped a man get out of China. My father had introduced me to someone back in Tennessee, a former communist, who'd come to America from China to attend a technology school. Because his English was poor, he somehow ended up at a *theology* school instead. Long story short, this man gave his life to Christ, earned a doctorate in theology, and became a missionary. His brother in China later became a Christian too, so the missionary wanted my help to get his brother out of the communist nation.

Leaving China, especially at that time, was not a simple matter. The brother also wanted to attend a theology school, but communist China doesn't roll like that. He apparently needed some documents in order to leave the country, and the missionary was convinced that if he mailed them to his brother they would never arrive.

That's where I came in.

I met with the missionary in Cleveland a couple of weeks before the trip. He handed me a manila envelope. "I need your help smuggling my brother out of China," he said. "Here's some paperwork for him." This missionary was a well-known Christian in China, someone who had known persecution and been warned not to return. I never opened the envelope, and he cautioned me that if I was discovered with the contents, it could lead to trouble for me and the group I was with.

This risky undertaking was exciting but also scary. I felt as if I were a "Mission Impossible" operative on a solo assignment behind enemy lines. No one else in the Lee Singers knew what I was doing. I successfully delivered the papers to this man's brother, and he eventually made it to America where he was able to attend seminary.

As I experienced these adventures, I started to develop a new mindset. "God," I said, "all I need is You." In fact, on the way back from China I told two of my traveling companions, "I don't think I'm ever going to get married. All I need in this world is my relationship with God."

That trip to China compelled me to look at other faith groups and how dedicated they are. Muslims around the world spend the entire Islamic month of Ramadan fasting from sunup to sundown and taking extra time in prayer and reflection. I thought about what would happen if Christians around the world fasted for a month. Since we worship the true God, the God of Abraham and Isaac, the God who sent us His son and created a new covenant with us, the God who hears us when we pray, how crazy good would that type of devotion be?

As I considered my time in China, I realized that I'd never personally humbled myself before God. After I came home, I got facedown on the ground before God to acknowledge that we're not equals. He's not my partner. He's not my buddy. He is God, and I'm His servant. That's what I want to be. That's what He created me to be.

Remember how I talked about the power of one positive choice? The choice to tell my friends that a relationship with Christ was more important than them led to utter isolation. That isolation led me to more time reading Scripture. The time I spent reading Scripture led to more time in prayer. More time in prayer led me to seeking God for new relationships.

Seeking godly relationships led me back to school. School led me back to the Lee Singers. The Lee Singers took me on a mission trip to China, and my experiences in China prepared me for what was next. My heart was ready. My spirit was ready.

I believe God brought me to that place of loneliness so He could prepare me for the next step. In fact, the day I returned to Wichita from China is the day I met my future wife. At the end of this lonely period, all of a sudden God rewarded me with the best friend I'll ever have. She came along at just the right time.

CHAPTER 6

KENDRA

———

I PRAYED FOR MY FUTURE WIFE throughout my high school years. I credit my mom for this, because she approached me one day to say she'd been thinking about the woman I would someday marry. "I feel like you should be praying for her," she said. Mom made herself clear, because she mentioned it a couple of times. *Mother knows best*, I figured, so I began praying for my future wife.

One day during my senior year, I was kneeling at the altar at Rolling Hills Church of God when someone on the ministry team came up beside me. As usual, I was praying for my wife: *God, protect her. Give her peace. Help her where she is in life. Whatever she's doing in her life right now, God, I'm lifting her up.* It was the same prayer almost every day.

This person kneeled down next to me, and the first thing I noticed was that she was crying. "Phil," she said. "I just got a word from God for you."

As I've said, the Church of God is a Pentecostal denomination, which means that sometimes someone will share a word of knowledge or a word of wisdom from the Lord. Yet I also know from experience that "speaking a word" into people's lives can cause heartache unless you've truly heard from God.

"What is it?" I asked.

"You've been praying for your future wife . . ." she began. I hadn't told anybody about this, so I thought, *This is for me from God. It's for me.*

"God wanted me to tell you," she continued, "that you're never going to have a wife because you're going to be too busy in ministry. He wants you to transfer your energy to praying for the ministry that He's giving you instead."

How did I react to this stunning revelation? Did I embrace this new plan for my life? Not exactly. I went out and had sex for the first time. And the second. And the third. I had remained pure until then, but that moment at the altar changed everything. It changed my focus and (obviously) my spiritual life.

Okay, God, I thought, *I'll receive this from You. But there's something in life that I'm not going to live without. . . .*

I didn't say this was a good decision. It clearly wasn't. I really wanted to be serious about my faith, but I was immature and kept getting pulled away by my poor choices. I don't blame that church worker for my actions, but I have learned to be extremely wary when others claim to be speaking on behalf of God. Personally, I avoid giving others "a word from God" unless an angel of the Lord shows up, and even then the Bible says that the devil can disguise himself as an angel of light. I guess I'm trying to say that people need to be really careful.

Because I received that word about not getting married as if it came directly from Jesus. It didn't.

———

Two of my best buddies during my senior year of high school were twins named Damon and Darren. When I returned home to Wichita for the summer after three weeks in China, Damon wanted me to meet Miranda, his new girlfriend.

By this time I'd accepted that I was never getting married, so I wasn't looking for a girlfriend. I was serious about my relationship with God, especially after my experiences in China, and why bother dating if you're never getting married?

That all changed when I knocked on Miranda's door. Her best friend, Kendra, answered, and I was attracted to her from the moment we met. We started talking, and it turned out that her father was also a pastor—for the Assemblies of God.

Kendra smiled—a lot. It wasn't just an everyday smile; she smiled so hard that her eyes almost shut. And she was beautiful! She was extremely smart and offered a witty comment for almost everything I said. We discussed everything from music to school to church. She told me about the terrible pain she experienced when her younger brother died in a car accident, and how her faith ultimately grew stronger as a result.

We connected on a deep level almost right away. On the day we met, we talked until nearly one o'clock in the morning. When I returned home, my father was still up playing solitaire. I told him that I'd met the girl I was going to marry. He just smiled.

Everyone thought we were crazy except our parents. When Kendra's father met me, he said, "This is the guy." He was soon making jokes about us having a home close to them some day. The night my mother met Kendra, she told Kendra that she was everything she'd ever prayed for in a daughter-in-law. We all knew early on that God had brought us together for a purpose. I think both Kendra and I knew instantly. We were married five months later.

What I didn't find out until later was that at the same time the high-school me was praying for my future wife—for peace, for help, for comfort—that's when Kendra's younger brother, Russell, was killed. God knew we were going to be together, and He put it on my heart to pray for someone I hadn't even met, right as she was going through the biggest heartbreak of her life.

Kendra had been planning to attend college in Oklahoma, but her father and I plotted and schemed and filled out an application for her at Lee University. She ended up with a presidential scholarship, because she's brilliant.

Some people thought Kendra was crazy to marry me. This girl was class president and homecoming queen. She was a 4.0 student. And then suddenly she married some nobody musician and ran off to Tennessee with him.

One of the first things she did was audition for the Lee Singers. She was accepted right away, and she thrived there. I thrived there too. After my little prodigal stint the year before, I came back and rejoined the group. In fact, I think Lee Singers might have been the only course I passed during my second semester, and I probably got a D.

Those first few years of marriage didn't always go smoothly. I loved being married to Kendra, and we loved each other deeply, but we didn't always like each other that much. She had it all together: She was Miss Lee University. She was president of her sorority. I, meanwhile, had nothing together. I wasn't particularly good at school. I slept in and missed classes.

It was fun being married, but we had real problems figuring out how to be married to each other.

It didn't help that Kendra was lonely because I worked a lot. When we were first married, I worked at McDonald's, and then I was hired at a factory. I only lasted one day at the factory. After that, I landed an engineering job at a recording studio. *Now I've made it*, I thought. *I can quit college!* But I was mistaken.

"No, you can't quit college," Kendra proclaimed. "I married a college student. I want to be married to a college graduate."

I knew I needed to make it to the finish line, but keep in mind that I'd never planned to attend college in the first place. I just wanted to be a musician. I might not have loved college, but it was during those years that I fell in love with overseas missions. Every summer, the Lee Singers took an international mission trip. We traveled to China and South Africa. We traveled to England, Scotland, and Wales. We traveled to the Caribbean. And on all of these trips, we shared the gospel with audiences through music.

I stuck it out at Lee, and by 2001 I became president of the choir. One guess who the vice president was. . . .

Kendra.

On one of these mission trips we were in South Africa. It was a dangerous trip, taken not long after the dismantling of apartheid. In Soweto they told us, "Don't even stop at the stoplights; they'll kill you just because you're white." Everywhere we went, we were instructed to be careful.

We ended up at a hotel I had booked for us that had no locks on the doors and people shooting up drugs in the hallways. It was quite a scene. I decided to set a curfew for all the choir members, and one night I remember poking Kendra awake. "Hey, it's your night to check curfew," I said, because all of the choir officers took turns checking curfew.

"I'm already asleep," she said.

Didn't she know who she was talking to? "I'm telling you—president to vice president—that you're going to get up and you're going to do this."

She looked back at me and replied, "And I'm telling you—wife to husband—no."

I eventually sought Dr. Mauldin's counsel that evening.

The Lee Singers' director was actually my mother's friend, and he became one of my life mentors. Almost everything I know about touring and singing I learned from him, but he taught me even more about marriage than music.

I showed up at Dr. Mauldin's hotel room around two o'clock in the morning. "I have to quit the Lee Singers," I announced, "because I feel like I have to choose either the Lee Singers or my marriage."

Dr. Mauldin set me straight. "Phil, your wife is smarter than you are," he said. "When she says something, listen to her." He explained that when a husband and wife both play to their strengths, they should be working together. In effect, he taught us how to be married, and we've had a wonderful marriage as a result.

By our last year in college, Kendra and I learned to work together in the choir. She focused on administration while I focused on the artistic aspects, including which songs we sang.

As Kendra and I discovered that I tend to be a creative and intuitive thinker and she tends to be analytical and logical, we learned how to better operate together instead of independently. For example, at the house I handled the cleaning; she handled the bills. In the choir, she took care of the structure and I took care of the music.

CHAPTER 7

IN THE NAVY

I CAN STILL REMEMBER THE DREAM. I was standing in a field, and in the middle of the field was a little house. I somehow knew—I don't know how to explain it, I just knew—that the house was a tomb. The dream was in black and white, but it felt very real and very personal.

I woke up in a sweat—perspiration streaming down my face—with Kendra wondering what in the world had happened.

That wasn't the end of it. The dreams continued for about two weeks, and every single night I would wake up screaming. In my dreams, I kept walking closer and closer to the house. One night I finally made it inside, and on the wall was a picture of Kendra. That's when I realized that the tomb was for my wife. At this point in time we were enjoying a renewed love for each other, and now I was dreaming about the loss of my wife. The next night, the walls of the home were covered with pictures of Kendra. The pictures were everywhere, and it felt like I'd lost her so many times. The pain was incredibly intense.

No surprise, by now I was having trouble sleeping. My dream, however, kept progressing. The next night it was in color for the first time. When I walked into the house, the room was red, like blood, and there were other pictures on the walls—not only of Kendra, but of faces I didn't recognize. At this point I was starting to freak out. Did I need to see a doctor? A therapist?

The very next morning, however, I woke up feeling refreshed. The bags under my eyes were gone, and Kendra commented, "You didn't wake up last night."

That's when we turned on the TV to see the news coverage of an airplane flying into the World Trade Center. It was the morning of September 11, 2001. I didn't make the correlation right away, but when the second plane hit and we realized it was a terrorist attack, I wondered if my dreams had been a warning.

Maybe the dreams were prompting me to pray; I wasn't sure. I've heard about other people having these sorts of premonitions. The news of the attack was on all the channels. You could see people jumping out of the buildings. It was psychologically jarring.

I went to class soon after the first tower came down, and then the university cancelled all remaining classes that day. The administration told us to go home and pray for our country. The entire nation became real patriotic, real fast. A few days later George W. Bush was there at Ground Zero, standing on the rubble with his megaphone, and suddenly you could relate to almost everybody on the street. Out in public, it felt like everyone was experiencing a sort of uniform pain. We grieved for the people who had lost loved ones, over the senseless violence in general, and for the senselessness of death in particular.

I was feeling it too, and I wanted to do something about it. Perhaps it was in my genes. After all, my father was a veteran; my grandfather had pictures of eagles and the American flag all over his walls. Country artists were especially feeling patriotic. Toby Keith quickly released a 9/11 song; so did Alan Jackson.

Meanwhile, I was in talks with a Christian record label, Sparrow Records, and they discussed signing me to a contract. They were looking for a big pop sound, for upbeat party music, and I was writing songs that fit that mold. Kendra was a public relations major, so she put together a media packet for me. I met with an A&R rep from Sparrow Records at a Gospel Music Association event, and he said, "Hey man, send me the press packet." When he heard my demo and saw all this promotional material, he said, "You may be the guy."

He brought me to Nashville for writing sessions and

recording sessions, and after I graduated from Lee in the spring of 2002, we immediately moved to Nashville. Kendra got a job at a car rental place, and I spent every day writing songs and working with this A&R rep on a potential contract.

My hopes for a music career were coming true. Throughout my life I'd said, "I'm going to be a singer. I'm going to be in music." I finally had a record deal on the table, but then . . . I ended up walking away. I wanted it to happen, I really did, but I wasn't comfortable with it on a spiritual level. We didn't feel at peace about the deal at all. I felt like an idiot when I walked away, but I knew God wasn't in this agreement. Of course, He had a better plan.

Kendra and I spent this season of life seeking God, but all the doors were shut for a music career. There was a music position at a Florida church; I interviewed with them and they loved me—until I mentioned my desire to be a record-ing artist. They responded, "Well, we don't need somebody here who's going to leave next year." After a while I started wondering if I wasn't going to be in music anymore. It was a devastating time. I questioned God: *If You're my source, if You're guiding me, why did You guide me here?*

I finally landed a job as a manager at a local rent-to-own business. I can't even explain how sad I was, because it was the first time I'd ever given up on music. Music had been my whole life. It wasn't my passion—Jesus is my passion;

God is my passion—but music was the only medium where I excelled. Music is what I'm good at. If you look at my toolbelt, music is my hammer and there are no other tools. At this point I felt lost and wondered what in the world I should do.

One day after the United States decided to invade Iraq, Kendra said to me, "Your country is something you're passionate about. You're so proud of your dad for being a veteran. Have you ever considered the military?"

"I didn't think you'd let me," I said.

I'd just been hired at the rent-to-own place, but I never worked a single day there. Instead I went with my wife to the local Marine recruiting center. The sign on the window said they were all at lunch. The Navy recruitment center was next door, so I walked in and asked, "How do I find information on becoming a naval officer, because I've got a college degree."

"What's your degree in?" they asked.

"It's in music."

"We don't have officer programs for music. You have to be enlisted in the music program."

That's when another man turned around and asked me, "Are you looking to be in the band?"

In the band? I'm a singer, so I don't think . . .

". . . because we have a position open for a singer."

I am not making this up.

The man was a senior chief petty officer, one of only three people in the entire country who could audition people to be in the Navy band by himself. What are the odds that he would be in the recruiting center that I visited that day? That's a God thing to me. I auditioned in a hotel conference room, and the officer put me in the Navy band. I sang a couple of cover songs for him and read some sheet music.

"All right," he said. "We'll put you into the delayed entry program. We've got a guy leaving next year who's a singer, and we need to replace him. That's going to be your job."

So I enlisted, but I didn't ship out until that position opened up.

We didn't know what being "in the band" actually meant. My dad was in a military band, but he ended up in Vietnam, so I wasn't sure that singing would keep me out of combat. I just thought the band was an appropriate place for me because music is my hammer.

I was ready to join up immediately, but Kendra had researched the process in advance and learned about available financial incentives the military offered if you enlisted. We kept bringing up the incentives to the recruiters, who said they didn't apply to musicians. That's when we walked out the first time. It was like haggling at a car dealership. Kendra negotiated my military contract on my behalf, and by the time we were done, my student loans were paid off, I received a signing bonus, and I had preferential placement for where I would end up. I had a five-year commitment up front, but the last year was optional. The whole process took a couple of weeks.

The night after that visit to the recruiting center, my

family attended a nearby revival service. (Some families go to movies; we go to revivals. We just wanted to be in church.) The minister called to me, motioned me forward, and looked me in the eye.

"You're a singer," he said.

"Yes, I am," I replied.

"I don't know what you did today," he said, "but God wants you to know that it was exactly what you needed to do. Today He didn't just open a door for you; He bulldozed down a wall for you. You thought you were going to be singing for churches, but now you're going to be singing for princes."

I already thought this Navy job was going to be cool. What I didn't realize was that the job would cause me to miss a buddy's wedding, which led to me auditioning for *American Idol*. And my success on *American Idol* has allowed me to sing for princes, presidents, and dignitaries all over the world. Therefore, I do believe that this minister had a message from God for me.

Because of the delayed-entry program, I didn't ship out until the fall of 2003. Kendra was pregnant with our first child by then, and it looked like she was going to have the baby while I was at boot camp. I wanted her to be around her parents, so we relocated to Shawnee, Oklahoma, where her dad was pastoring a church.

Mark and Tami McIntosh are my in-laws, and we've always been close. We moved into a house near theirs, and I worked at a church pastored by one of Mark's friends. I finally shipped out to boot camp in Great Lakes, Illinois, about forty-five minutes outside of Chicago. Boot camp lasted for two months, and I didn't come home until December 2003.

The toughest part about boot camp was the separation from my wife. Our first child, Chloe, was born on October 31. The recruiters told me I could be with my family when our baby arrived, but that wasn't the case. Kendra tried to help bring me back to Oklahoma by conspiring with the hospital nurses. They told the Navy that Chloe had a medical condition, which she did.

The Navy still didn't let me come home. On top of that, the only message I received via the command center was that there were complications with the baby, and hearing that made me freak out with worry. When I was finally able to call home, I learned that Chloe had some jaundice, which I discovered is fairly normal among newborns.

Kendra and Chloe traveled to Great Lakes for my graduation, so that's when I was able to hold Chloe for the first time. You're often told as a parent that you're going to have this instant bond with your child, but that wasn't the case with us. Part of the reason was that she'd been alive for over a month and I hadn't been there for any of it. After my graduation we were stationed in Virginia Beach, Virginia, so from that point on I asked Kendra to let me get up in the night with Chloe. I'd already missed out on the miracle of birth; I wasn't going to fall any further behind as a father. Chloe and I had to work at it, but over time we developed such a wonderful and strong father-daughter bond.

We spent six or seven months in Virginia Beach, and I joined the worship team at a local church. I was pretty sure that I was called to ministry, but I didn't know what that meant anymore. Did it mean pursuing vocational ministry as my father and mother did? I was in the Navy now, and I had never experienced anything like it.

After Virginia Beach, I was stationed in Jacksonville, Florida, at Naval Air Station Jacksonville. We lived near the beach, and I was assigned to a rock band—a Navy rock band. It was a great place for career musicians.

My unit was categorized as ceremonial, which meant I sang the national anthem when the admiral spoke. I sang at Jacksonville Jaguars football games, at Jacksonville Suns baseball games, and at colleges and other local events. But my primary job was the rock band, which meant traveling around to high schools.

During the recruitment push for Navy SEALs, we often traveled with members of a SEAL unit. We were usually on the road for a couple of weeks at a time, performing at high schools throughout the Southeast. We played modern rock songs—music from bands including Yellowcard, My Chemical Romance, and Fall Out Boy—and on the weekends we performed at military balls where we played mostly classic rock hits and dance music.

I was the main vocalist in the band, and there were definitely times when I didn't sing well. Even so, I improved quite a bit during those years, especially compared to my college performances. In the Navy I learned more about my voice, because they want you to sound like the artist you're covering. If you're singing Sinatra, you need to sound like Sinatra. If you're singing Guns N' Roses, you need to sound like Axl Rose. I figured out how to manipulate my voice to sound a certain way. It was an intense training time, musically speaking.

———

With a steady Navy salary to support us, we decided to buy a car. Chloe was still an infant, and back then I enjoyed making silly family videos. One of them I called "A Day in the Life," which included a five-minute segment of me showing off the car. It was a white 2001 Mazda Millenia with brown leather interior and a sunroof. *I got myself a sweet ride*, I thought. Yes, the car was pretty nice, but I was pretty foolish at the time.

We'd owned the car for barely a month when we met up with some buddies from college. They were in the area for a concert, and we went out for a drive after the show. I was behind the wheel with my college buddy Chad in the passenger seat and Kendra and Chloe in the back.

"What do you think of my ride?" I asked.

"It's great, Phil," Chad said. "Good job."

"I love this car, man," I said. "I love this car more than the ring that I proposed to my wife with."

I was being slaphappy and silly, and I was just getting started.

"I love this car more than the roof I put over my daughter's head."

Okay, so I'm not the world's funniest comedian.

"I love this car more than my copy of the Holy Bible."

I don't know why I said those foolish things, but nobody was laughing anymore. Chad just stared at me.

"I just cursed my car, didn't I?" I asked.

"Yeah," Chad said. "I think you did."

Right as he said those words, we came to a red light. As I came to a stop behind the car in front of us, I felt a jolt and heard the sickening sound of crushing metal. The drunk driver behind us plowed into the back of our car and sandwiched us between his vehicle and the one in front of us. None of us in the Mazda were injured at all—not a scratch on us—but the car was demolished. Totaled. The front end was gone. The back end was gone. My baby girl, however, slept through the entire thing.

The drunk driver was able to climb out of his car. The guy in front of us wasn't injured either, but his car was also a wreck. I tell that story because my mother used to say, "Be careful what you say." I had just said something that wasn't true, putting my car in a position of honor even above the Word of God.

From a legal perspective, I know I didn't cause the

accident. But in my heart, I felt as if it were my fault because I was an idiot. The cops arrived and charged the guy behind us, but I learned to be careful with the words I say.

I took a part-time job as a worship pastor while I was in the Navy. We weren't always traveling, so I could usually lead worship at a church on Sundays. I also started pursuing my music career again in Jacksonville for the first time since we'd left Nashville. Being a Navy singer opened doors for me to sing in more churches. I set up a recording studio in my house, and my buddies were all singer/songwriters. God has always given me friends who influenced me to continue in music. The music minister at my church had attended the same college as me, so we clicked instantly.

I've never been a prolific songwriter, but I've always written songs. One of my best-known songs, "Old Glory"—first recorded by the Navy band and later covered by several others—was written while I was in the service. I was inspired to write it after a ceremony where I sang the national anthem. There were people at the event who were legit military heroes, and meeting them and some of the wounded warriors gave me a new perspective.

I was never deployed to a combat zone, and I never went to the Middle East. I went instead to numerous high schools, recruiting other people to the combat zone. Serving in the band, I tended to forget that my comrades were fighting a war.

There were five members in the band, including me. It was a good group, and we had so much fun together. Some of the song lyrics, however, were a bit questionable and dealt with sex and suicide. At one point I asked my commanding officer, who was also a Christian, "Are you comfortable with us singing some of this material in high schools?" After he read some of the lyrics, he said, "I'm going to need your approval on lyrics before you take them to high schools." From that point on I had to okay all of our lyrics.

I didn't want to be a prude, and I sometimes feared I would be perceived that way. One of my bandmates was a devout atheist, and we had conversations where he tried to stir me up, tried to make me upset. We were buddies, but if I got riled up he could say, "See, that's what I'm talking about. That's what Christians are really like." I did my best to not be judgmental or come across as prudish. The most prudish thing I did was decide that we couldn't sing certain songs.

My Christian friends didn't know about the music I was performing. I'm not sure they would have cared. But I definitely had a problem with singing about suicide in high schools, because if you're considering suicide, I want to help you. I want to be a force for good in the lives of young people.

Some people in the band considered that time to be our glory years. We were getting paid to tour like a rock band; we had big lights and sound systems like a rock band; and we had built-in audiences everywhere. It was a rock musician's dream come true. We ate nice food and stayed in hotels on the beach for days at a time. I think we began to believe that we *were* rock stars, and I felt I had to remind everyone that we were also representatives of the U.S. Navy. We performed in our uniforms, after all, which is kind of funny when you think about it.

At the same time, our audiences definitely had fun. We'd crowd surf in high schools. The kids went crazy. My bandmates were all skilled musicians, and I was relatively good at what I did, but I didn't consider our performances as my special time in life. I was busy building a family. I already had one child and was way more into being a dad. Don't get me wrong: I loved my position in the Navy band. Many of the sailors stationed in Jacksonville were crazy busy; they had work to do every single day. But I was in the band, so I didn't. There were times where I'd go to work at 9:30 a.m. and come home by noon because there was really nothing to do.

Our church in Jacksonville had a profound effect on me. The guys I worked with there—Larry Kusic, his brother Donnie Kusic, and Adam Marcum—were also creative and loved to play music. God gave me these guys as friends, and we would get together to sing and write songs. All three of them inspired me to continue writing and performing. In fact, Donnie ended up coming with me to my *American Idol* audition.

CHAPTER 8

AUDITION TIME

THE NAVY BAND was great preparation for *American Idol* because I was exposed to a lot of different types of music. (There's not much gospel music on *American Idol*.)

While I was in the Navy, *American Idol* was becoming more and more popular. During season five, when *Idol* contestant Chris Daughtry made it to the final four, I'd be performing somewhere in Florida and people would comment on our resemblance: "Didn't I just see you on television last night?"

I never imagined participating in a show like *American Idol*—ever. Never even considered it. When you're a singer, plenty of people tell you, "You should do *American Idol*," but

I couldn't picture performing in front of that many people. Sure, I was fairly comfortable onstage, but not with a camera in my face!

The show was big in part because of a British judge named Simon Cowell who often made fun of the performers— telling them how bad they were. I didn't want to hear that. I'd already had a negative experience with that in high school, and college wasn't necessarily easy. In the Navy band, folks got on me for not sounding exactly like Axl Rose. I'd had enough criticism; I didn't need any more of that in my life. Yet I think God used all those experiences to prepare me for *American Idol*.

The audition only happened because I was on one of those high school tours—a conflict that forced me to miss my friend Bart Norton's wedding. After the tour was over, I called him and apologized: "Man, I'm so sorry that I couldn't make it."

"Well, there's one way I would forgive you," he said. "They're doing *American Idol* auditions. I just want to see that you auditioned."

This was in 2006. I was twenty-eight years old, which is the age cutoff for *American Idol*. That same summer, the Church of God had a general assembly in Indianapolis, which is like a national convention, and I attended to perform with the Lee Singers. Kendra and I had car trouble in Indianapolis, but we didn't have money for the repairs. That's when we saw a karaoke bar with a sign out front: "Cash Award." Dr. Mauldin was with us, so we all went inside. The prize for winning was $500, and I won! More important, it was enough money to pay for our car repairs. Dr. Mauldin looked at me and asked, "Have you ever considered auditioning for *American Idol?*"

"Bart Norton wants me to try out," I said.

"Maybe you should. You just won a karaoke contest."

Kendra and I talked about it, and I said, "What if it did happen? What if I did get on this show? That would be super dope, because I just won $500. Yesterday I couldn't afford to fix the car, and today I can, so why don't I go?"

I asked my commanding officer back in Jacksonville if I could try out for the show. He said, "Sure, why not?"

The nearest *American Idol* audition for season six was in Memphis, Tennessee, on September 2 at the FedExForum. Kendra was pregnant with our second child, so Donnie Kusic went with me.

Donnie and I had a blast. About 16,000 people showed up for the audition, but we didn't register ahead of time like many contestants did. We pulled up at three o'clock in the morning after driving all night, and people were already standing in line. We walked around the arena and said to each other, "How cool would it be if we met *the* American Idol?"

We talked with as many people as possible while the organizers started the auditions. I made some new friends that day, some of whom I still hear from. It was a huge cattle call.

Judges sat at tables all over the building, and they brought people up four at a time to each table. Each contestant probably had about ten seconds to impress a judge.

Donnie and I finally got our chance to sing at around 10:30 that night. Back then, people probably thought that everyone auditioned in front of Simon Cowell, Paula Abdul, and Randy Jackson. We certainly thought so at first, but as soon as we saw the crowds we realized that wasn't going to happen. They had to narrow down the field. A lot.

When at last they brought four of us up to a table, I was at one end and Donnie was at the other. By this late in the day, the judges had been instructed to not let anybody else through unless they were special. We saw great singers get rejected.

After we sang, the woman judging us said, "You two in the middle, I think you should come back next year. This isn't the season for you. But you two"—she pointed to Donnie and me—"I'm thinking about picking one of you guys to go through."

Donnie and I looked at each other and he started crying. It couldn't be any more perfect. The judge didn't know we were friends, and when we told her she asked how we knew each other. "We're in a Christian rock band together," we said. (Our group was called My Dear Theophilus, though we rarely actually performed together.)

"Then I'm sending both of you through," she said. This meant we had to remain in town for another two days. We met the two executive producers, and I called Kendra to see if we had money for a hotel room. Unfortunately, we really didn't, so Donnie and I ended up staying at the Navy base in nearby Millington, Tennessee.

I had to call my commanding officer.

"Sir, I need a couple of days extension," I told him. "I got through." Neither of us had planned for this. We'd never discussed what would happen if my audition was successful. My CO was frantic—the United States Navy would not be happy if I appeared on *American Idol* without their knowledge.

Josh Gracin, a U.S. Marine, had competed on the second season of *American Idol*, and there was so much drama surrounding his participation that I think the military preferred to not go through that again. Josh finished fourth that season, but he wasn't able to join the *American Idol* tour because he had to finish his military commitment. My CO knew about that, and he told me, "You can stay in Memphis for the next couple of days, Phil, but I don't know if this is something you can do."

We stayed, and Donnie was cut in the next round. If you've ever watched *American Idol*, you know that they like it when the contestants have some sort of interesting personal story. My first story was that I was in a rock band with a fellow contestant. After Donnie was eliminated, my story became that I was in the Navy.

Once the judges let me through, they said, "Go home and we'll contact you about the next audition. You're going to sing for Randy, Simon, and Paula."

I was supposed to be in Memphis on October 5 for the next audition. I initially told the *Idol* producers, "I don't think I can do it. My wife is nine months pregnant."

"You'll only be gone for one day," they reassured me. "We'll have you back before you know it."

Kendra was actually okay with it. "You've made it through multiple rounds," she said. "You could go to Hollywood."

By this time my commanding officer had received approval for my participation.

I'd already missed the birth of one child, and I felt bad enough about that. I didn't think I should go to Memphis . . . Kendra was telling me I should . . . so I agreed to sing for the judges and return home right away. This time my father and my brother met me in Memphis. (If you watch the clip of my audition, you can see the two of them running with me at the end.)

I was awakened in my Memphis hotel room by a 4:00 a.m. phone call. It was my mother, who had gone to Jacksonville to stay with Kendra. "Philip, guess who's here?" she said, and I could hear a baby crying in the background. My second daughter, McKayla, was born on the morning of my big audition.

I went to the audition area and waited for the producers to show up. "I just want to let you know I'm not going to audition today," I told them. "I have to go back home because my baby was just born. We didn't think she was going to arrive for a couple of weeks."

"Hold on a second," they urged. They could smell a good story, and a camera crew quickly appeared to interview me. They immediately moved me to the front of the line; I was the first person to audition for the judges in Memphis.

It's not my favorite term, but in show business slang the last person to go on in a talent show is said to have the pimp spot, because everybody is going to remember your performance. As long as you don't mess up, you're golden. I didn't have that luxury; I auditioned first. I don't remember much about it, but I do remember it being really quiet. The room was full of crew members—about seven or eight other people in addition to the judges. The whole experience was kind of surreal. It's like you're inside the television; you're finally singing for the three famous judges. I had already met host Ryan Seacrest, and that was cool, but he was outside in the hallway. Once inside the room, I was on my own.

Production workers were everywhere. They knew things about the contestants that . . . I don't even know how to explain it. I once made an offhand remark that an *American Idol* staffer brought up weeks later. I remember thinking, *How do they know that about me?* The crew was watching us; people were paying attention behind the scenes. By the time I walked into the audition room, the judges already knew about McKayla's birth.

"Where's my cigar, dog?" asked Randy Jackson.

"Are you happy?" asked Paula Abdul.

"I'm ecstatic," I replied.

"What's more important," asked Simon Cowell, "getting through to Hollywood or the baby?"

I could only smile and shake my head. "Sorry, man—the baby's more important to me."

"Weird," said Simon. "Now that's weird."

What would the audience have thought of me if I'd told Simon the audition was more important? It would have been silly. Of course I wasn't going to say that, even if I had felt that way. But I didn't feel that way. My new baby *was* more important to me than a singing competition.

Simon's reaction indicated that, at least in his mind, *American Idol* should have been my priority. I think Simon's life changed dramatically a few years later when he had a baby of his own. When you have a child, you understand life differently. It doesn't matter who you are—your priorities change when you're a parent.

Unfortunately, my mind wasn't with my audition at all. Suddenly it didn't seem very important. I thought it was cool that I was singing for Paula Abdul, because she was the biggest thing since sliced bread when I was in middle school, but I wasn't present mentally. I could hardly remember what song I'd planned to do. I'd made a joke earlier that morning about singing Marvin Gaye's "Let's Get It On," but it's basically a song about sex. I'm a church guy; I wasn't going to sing that. I settled on "My Girl" by the Temptations in honor of my three girls back home. That's an appropriate song, I figured, especially considering that I'd just had a daughter.

I proceeded to sing for the judges, and I didn't sound great. Not a shock. After all, I'd been up since 4:00 a.m.

The judges' reactions were mixed. "I wish I could have heard something else," Paula said.

Seizing the opportunity, I immediately started singing again. I didn't think, I just *did*. What came out of my mouth? "Let's Get It On."

Sometimes your brain just stops functioning in these situations. You have no idea how you're being perceived. You know how there are always some contestants each season who are obviously poor singers? I remember wondering for a moment if I might be a joke, if I might be one of those "bad" auditions.

I wasn't near the judges at all, probably twenty feet away. It was a big room, with them on one side and me near the opposite wall. I didn't shake their hands, and I could barely hear them, especially when they were talking to each other. They had microphones so that the television audience could hear them perfectly, but I couldn't.

I managed to sing about ten seconds' worth of Marvin Gaye before Randy and Simon started arguing about my performance. Randy liked me; Simon was completely unconvinced. Paula was the tie breaker, and she told me I was going to Hollywood. I have a vague memory of a producer handing me a golden ticket as I walked out of the room.

Once I left the audition room, it was like I was back in the real world—especially with Ryan Seacrest waiting there, because he's just so normal, such a regular person. But I didn't want to hang around and chat. Sure, I'd made it to Hollywood, but I'd missed my baby's birth—again. I had a newborn girl I was desperate to see. I ran right out of there, even though it was another two hours before I could get a flight home.

Back then the show didn't try to capture every moment like it does now, but the producers still gave us a video camera to take with us back to Jacksonville. As a result, the moment I met McKayla was shown on *American Idol*, which is definitely cool.

I don't have any evidence of this, but it's my guess that the *Idol* judges had a pretty good idea in advance which contestants they would put through. They probably had the ability to revisit those decisions on the fly, but I don't think they would have spent so much time interviewing the guy who missed the birth of his baby and then not send me to Hollywood.

I've concluded that the judges were always looking for *interesting* singers. When contestants make it through in the early rounds, I think the judges base the decision, at least in part, on whether they're interesting to watch on television. Because not all good singers are interesting to watch.

At first I was considered interesting because Donnie and I were in a group together. Then I was interesting because I was in the Navy. Then I suddenly had a newborn. The show devoted plenty of screen time to my story.

Back then, *American Idol* was run by really good people. They were nice. They were kind. At the same time, they weren't particularly friendly to gospel music. I remember that one of the executive producers said, "If you sing a Christian song, we're not going to air you. If you try to use this as an opportunity to preach the gospel to people, nobody's ever going to hear you, and we're not going to send you through to Hollywood, so you might as well not do it." Of course, they actually have aired a few Christian songs, so he was just trying to discourage it.

Returning to Jacksonville was like re-entering the real world. I was back with my family, back in the Navy band. But my relationship with the Navy band members shifted. When I made it on *American Idol*, my bandmates gave me a hard time because I was leaving the group. After three years together they would have to deal with somebody else. In their minds, the glory days were over. They did an interview with MTV, joking about how bitter they were, but these were some of my best friends at the time and some of them are still good buddies today.

The Navy decided to re-station me in California if I made it on the show, so now I had to complete tons of forms. Kendra was going to remain in Jacksonville because we didn't think I was going to make it very far on the show. Neither of us thought I would last past Hollywood Week.

Simon didn't like my audition, but at least I had Hollywood Week. I was going to be on television!

CHAPTER 9

HOLLYWOOD

―――――

I HAD FOUR WEEKS to prepare before heading to Hollywood. In that time, I started listening to Clay Aiken's music. Clay was the runner-up on season two of *American Idol*, and I thought he had the best voice I'd ever heard on the show. "I need to learn to sing like Clay Aiken," I said, "and then I'm going to do okay."

Clay has what's known as an "open" voice, which means he relaxes his throat when he sings, giving him more power. His notes are clearer and stronger because of that.

I was friends with a record producer named James Matchack, and I went to Atlanta so we could get into a studio and James could train me to sound like Clay. If I can imitate Robert Plant from Led Zeppelin, I figured, then I can certainly imitate Clay Aiken. I can't sound like season two winner Ruben Studdard; that's just not going to happen. I can't be season five's Chris Daughtry, either, because Chris had a shaved head like me. If I tried to sound like Chris, I would get pushed to the side immediately because his career was already taking off.

I kept listening to Clay Aiken even after I got to Hollywood. I don't remember much about actually arriving in Los Angeles, but I do remember everyone piling on to several buses. On that first day, all the contestants sang onstage, and later that same day they dismissed probably half the field. Some of the people they let go were so talented—it blew my mind.

The day began with what seemed like a couple of hundred people. (I can't say for sure, but the theater we were in was about half full.) They had us stand in a line, and each contestant would step out, sing a song, then step back. Everything was sung a cappella, and afterward they called out numbers, since we all had numbers on our shirts. They separated us into two groups, a front line and a back line, before dismissing one of the lines. Sometimes it was the front line, sometimes the back. You didn't know until they said, "Back line, you made it through." It felt as if they did it that way just to mess with us, but I made it through.

The next day, the show took all the guys out on the town. We went to the beach and took a trolley around Hollywood. We made new friends. I met several of the eventual finalists that day, including Chris Richardson and Sanjaya Malakar. I met Blake Lewis, who was the runner-up my season, and Jason Head, whom everyone called Sundance. (Sundance was eliminated during the semifinals of *Idol*, but he wasn't done competing. In 2016 he won season eleven of *The Voice*.)

While the guys were out on the town, the girls were singing for the judges. Once again they called out numbers and rows. Once again numerous good singers were dismissed. The next day it was reversed, and a bunch of amazing guys were sent home. After the guys' round, at the end of the day, they brought us all together.

"Congratulations," they said. "You've made it through to the group round."

For the group round they gave us a selection of songs to choose from. "You need to find a group," they instructed, "and your group needs to sing for us tomorrow morning."

I ended up in a group with two pastors and a teenage girl. One of the pastors had been in prison before. They both had great stories, and one of them, Sean Michel, is still a dear friend. He had a long, bushy beard back then, and it's even longer now. He's a great singer, and when he auditioned for *American Idol*, Sean sang "God's Gonna Cut You Down" by Johnny Cash. During his audition interview, he said, "Everybody says I look like either Osama Bin Laden, or Jesus, or [Fidel] Castro, or just a homeless bum. But really, I think all of us are kind of homeless. When it comes down to it, all of us are really poor inside."

Our group chose the old sixties hit "Da Doo Ron Ron." All the groups were feeling the pressure to add choreography, to do harmony parts, and everyone had to sing lead on a verse. We stayed up all night practicing.

I'm not sure if all of the contestants realized it, but the judges were testing us on our memorization skills. You don't have much time to learn new songs on *American Idol*, so the producers want to make sure they have performers who won't forget the lyrics during the live shows. I think I was the only one in our group who remembered all the lyrics. They let Sean go that day as well as the teenage girl. The other guy, Justin, stayed until later in the week. Two of us made it through, but I was super sad because Sean was becoming a buddy.

Blake Lewis was in a group with Rudy Cardenas, Thomas Lowe, and Chris Sligh—who was my roommate that week—and they sang the Bee Gees' "How Deep Is Your Love" in what might be the best group round performance of all time. At one point Blake started beat-boxing, and I was blown away. That day I thought, *I'm not going to make it very far in this competition.* I was listening to the other singers and thinking how crazy good they were.

That same evening they brought us together and gave us another choice of songs, this time just a handful, to perform as individuals. It was the performance when Simon Cowell finally said he liked me. I chose "Have You Ever

Really Loved a Woman?" by Bryan Adams, and when I finished, Paula turned to Simon and said, "That was the best he's ever done."

"By a mile," Simon replied.

For the first time all week, my roommate Chris said, "Hey man, it looks like you might make it through."

But people were still getting cut left and right. If you think the people who made it to the live singing rounds were good, you should have seen the people eliminated during Hollywood Week! Way before we should have, we said goodbye to some of the best vocalists I'd ever heard. Yet little things like forgetting lyrics or having one subpar performance made even great singers targets for elimination.

The judges knew that if a performer was shaky during these rounds, the pressure of live TV could lead to the sort of on-air breakdown that generates negative publicity for the show. Anyone who missed a lyric was automatically at risk. Many people can sing, but *American Idol* was looking for star performers who could handle the pressure. Good singers, after all, are a dime a dozen.

By week's end, the contestants numbered about sixty, and the last thing they did was separate us into three hotel rooms. My room included people I barely recognized at all, so I figured, *Okay, our room is getting eliminated.* The next step was narrowing the group down to the top forty. The suspense was intense.

It seemed like we waited there for hours. And then Randy, Simon, and Paula finally walked in. Of course they made a show of it: *Hey guys—long day, long week. Did you have fun?* *We hope you've had fun, because we wanted you to have a good experience. We think you're all so talented, and we thank you so much for coming to Hollywood. The trip was on us. Hope you enjoyed it.*

I thought about how much fun it had been. It was an unforgettable experience, and I'd surely met the *American Idol* winner because I'd met just about everybody. By now I was convinced that our room would be cut.

"I should just put you out of your misery now, right?" said Randy. "I'm really sorry to say that . . ."

There was a dramatic "reality show pause." Some people were crying quietly.

". . . you guys are going to see a lot more of us. You're through."

The room exploded in a mixture of joy and relief. Sanjaya was in my room; Sundance too. Sanjaya's sister, however, was in the room that got eliminated. By then I was friends with both Sanjaya and Shyamali, and when we left the room Sanjaya immediately ran to her. Shyamali was bawling; everybody from that room was crying. At that point they sent everybody home with the understanding that the top forty would return to Los Angeles in January.

When you make it through to the next round on *American Idol*, you can't tell anyone outside of your family. They want the results to be a secret until that episode airs, so you have to keep them absolutely confidential. But not everyone did.

After we survived Hollywood Week, one contestant went to the *Florida Times-Union* and told them I had made it through. They did a story on it, and it started showing up on numerous spoiler websites: "Phil Stacey definitely made it." That's when *American Idol* contacted me and dropped me from the show.

It wasn't just my name; one website published a whole list of contestants who'd made it through. I think a couple of them were wrong, but this unknown source had most of the names correct. When the news got out that I'd made it, the show called me. "We're not going to need you to come back in January," they said. They thought I'd talked to the press after I had agreed not to.

It was devastating news, but I enjoyed the Navy and I still had my position as a worship leader. Between those two jobs, I was making better money than I'd ever made in my life, so I began to wonder if maybe it was for the best.

My family agreed that I'd had a great run, and none of us had anticipated that I would make it this far anyway. Nobody in my life had said, "Phil, you could win it all." Not a single person. But I wasn't ready to give up. Not yet. I needed to convince the producers that I wasn't the leaker, so I got on the phone.

"Guys, I wouldn't sabotage this for myself," I said, "but I will tell you that anybody in my Navy band could have leaked it, because there's no way I could leave without telling the Navy. Other people can just quit their jobs or tell people at the last minute, but I can't."

It took a couple of weeks, but they finally called and told me I could come back after all. I had my theories about who the source was, but I couldn't prove it.

In January 2007, all the contestants arrived back in Los Angeles, where they put us in a hotel. Yet before we sang another note, there was some unfinished business to attend to.

It felt great to be in the top forty, but we all knew that just twenty-four contestants—twelve guys, twelve girls—would participate in the live shows. By the time we returned to California, the judges had reviewed footage of our performances. Each of us would go before the judges alone. No more singing, no more chances to impress. One by one we took an elevator up to the second floor of the Pasadena Civic Center, where Simon, Paula, and Randy were waiting at a table at the end of a long room. One by one we each made the nerve-wracking walk across the polished wood floor to a single chair in front of that table.

That's where the judges revealed each contestant's fate. We called that episode the Green Mile—named after the death row walk that condemned prisoners took in the book and movie of the same name.

It was emotional torture. As far as I know, the Green Mile operates differently in each season, since each season has its own personality. I can reveal that they had us all undergo a psychological evaluation. We were all in town for a few days, staying in a hotel, before they recorded the Green Mile episode. We were all secluded from society while they evaluated us mentally.

At the time I thought it was weird. In retrospect, however, I can see why they did it. They also tried to uncover any potential controversies: *Are there any naked pictures of you out there? Do you have any felonies?* They either wanted to avoid scandal or use it for publicity; I'm not sure which. It's a television show, after all. Let's not pretend that the entertainment industry has only wholesome intentions.

I think they wanted to avoid putting anybody on the show who was mentally unstable. They brought in two psychologists, a man and a woman, and we each met individually with them twice over four days. The sessions probably lasted an hour or two, and they asked a lot of questions about our upbringing and home life—*tell us about your family*, that sort of thing.

It makes complete sense to me now, because competing on *American Idol* is a form of intense psychological trauma. Think about it: You're a performer who just wants to entertain people, and now you're on a hugely popular television show where you're criticized before millions of viewers. It's an opportunity for every critic on the internet to decide how bad you are, and the judges could find something negative to say about virtually everyone. They even bashed Carrie Underwood, who is one of the best singers I've ever heard.

I still didn't grasp just how huge the show was, or that I'd be reading about it in *USA Today* if I performed poorly. I just thought it would be fun. All I knew for sure was that I was on *American Idol*!

When it was my turn to walk the Green Mile, I still thought it would be okay if I was eliminated. Kendra and I had settled it in our minds that *American Idol* wouldn't become *the* big thing for us. But then it was. Once again, the judges played up the suspense for the cameras.

"It's definitely moment of truth time," said Randy. "I remember at the Memphis audition. you missed the birth of your daughter, right?"

"I did."

"So, are you ready for the truth?" he asked.

"I'm ready."

"Dude, you made it. You're through to the next round. You're on the show, baby!"

Watching that episode, you can see the relief wash over my face. *I made it to the top twenty-four out of 100,000 contestants!* I couldn't believe it.

From that point on, everything that happened to me would soon be seen by millions of viewers. However, I couldn't talk about any of it with the outside world. We weren't allowed on social media. Back then social media was MySpace—Facebook and Twitter had recently launched, but they weren't very popular yet.

Once the judges narrowed the field to twenty-four semi-finalists, that's when the season six episodes started airing. Because each season always begins with the airing of regional audition episodes, I spent several evenings in a hotel room with some of the other semifinalists, watching how our auditions went. Some days we took out guitars and sang together. We were just having fun. Then the Green Mile episode aired, and the next week we were on.

In the days leading up the live shows, everyone met with the *Idol*-affiliated record label. They brought in a lawyer who described the process to us: "You're all getting record deals. Every one of you." If you made it to the top twelve, you received a nice advance on a recording contract. If you made it to top five, you made even more, because every week you recorded a new song for fans to purchase online.

They wanted us to sign these contracts as well as a management deal with 19 Entertainment—the same company that produces *American Idol*. There are a lot of *Idol* contestants who say they were ripped off. Nonsense. It wasn't a bad deal. After all, we were nobodies before *Idol*. Then suddenly, we were singing in front of millions. All things considered, they gave us a pretty fair shake. Carrie Underwood stayed with that label for many years. And if you didn't want to sign the contract, you were free to go. They knew plenty of other performers who would love to have that opportunity. Everyone signed.

Once we made it to the live shows, we were allowed to choose our own songs, which the producers then had to get cleared. My songs for the semifinals were "I Could Not Ask for More" by Edwin McCain, "Missing You" by John Waite, and "I Need You" by LeAnn Rimes. All of them were suggested by my producer friend James Matchack, who helped me achieve a bigger singing voice.

I was brand new to singing in that style, so I was experimenting with it on television. Sometimes it worked, and sometimes it didn't. Tuesday night arrived, and it was time for the top twelve guys to sing. On live TV. Kendra was in the audience that night, and they probably cut to her at least a half dozen times.

I remember the moment when I was standing onstage and that little red light came on. I went last—the pimp spot. The producers usually placed the best performer in the closing slot, and that night they put me on last. I sang "I Could Not Ask for More," but something happened when that little red light came on. At that moment, I somehow knew that I didn't want to be famous. My whole life I wanted to be a singer, and in one fell swoop I knew I didn't want fame.

Why not? What changed?

I did not like all those eyes on me. I felt uncomfortable. *I don't know anything. People are going to think I know things. People are going to ridicule me. Is this how I want to make it? If I do make it, do I really want to be an* American Idol *guy? Is it too late for me to walk off the stage?* Still, I kept singing.

The beginning was rough, but then I hit my stride and finished strong. The judges gave me fairly good reviews; Paula and Randy both loved my performance. In fact, Randy said I was the best vocal of the night, and the director cut to a beaming Kendra. Simon was critical, as usual, and Ryan Seacrest finally asked him why he was so negative. "I don't believe in lying," Simon replied. I mostly just stood there nodding. All I wanted was to get off the stage.

Wednesday night was the women's turn, and they just killed us. The girls were so much better than the guys, and the pimp spot went to LaKisha Jones. She sang "And I Am Telling You I'm Not Going." Her performance was incredible. After LaKisha finished, Simon said, "I am very tempted to say to twenty-three [other] people: 'Book your plane tickets home.' That was in a different league." He would not always be so complimentary to the contestants.

CHAPTER 10

LIFE ON *IDOL*

THURSDAY NIGHT was the first live elimination episode. The set included a circular holding room overlooking the stage that we called the Coke Room because it was sponsored by Coca-Cola. It's where the contestants waited for our turn to sing during the semifinals and where we did interviews with Ryan Seacrest. We watched each other's performances from our perch in the Coke Room.

As we sat in this room, I remember thinking: *I want to get eliminated. If I make it further than this, I'm going to start wanting it. And if I start wanting it, that's bad because I probably can't have it.*

I didn't yet realize that God had a sovereign plan for me. I didn't realize that He would make it work in my favor. I did think to myself, *If He wants me to win, I'm going to win, and there is nothing in heaven or hell that can stop it if God wants it to happen.* (Of course, He could also empower my voice to sound like Pavarotti if He wanted to, but that didn't happen!) I was in God's hands, and He had a plan that I didn't see at the time.

Two guys and two girls were eliminated that first week, reducing the roster to twenty. After I made it through, Kendra started getting calls from people we knew in Kentucky, Ohio, Kansas—everywhere. The producers gave all the contestants new cell phones, and the only calls I was allowed to answer were theirs, so people flooded Kendra's phone with messages. That's when we decided to have her stay in Los Angeles.

Maybe we were a little too confident too soon, but hadn't I earned the pimp spot for the first live show? What's more, I received probably the best compliments that night. Now, I didn't really think I was going to win the whole thing, but at that point I was hoping to do pretty well.

So Kendra stayed in LA even though *American Idol* was the most anti-marriage environment you could possibly imagine. They didn't want families together. If you were married, they wanted to keep you apart. My wife was not allowed in my room. When she first came out to Hollywood, she moved in with a high school buddy of mine and his roommates just so she could be with me. Our daughters took turns staying with us, each girl for a week at a time, while the other daughter would stay with Kendra's parents in Oklahoma.

On top of that, every week more people wanted to visit us and see the show. *American Idol* only allotted us a certain number of seats each week, so we had to choose which folks we were going to invite. My mom had priority, of course, but we also welcomed visits from friends and extended family, including my Aunt Linda and her daughter Michelle. Kendra coordinated all of that, and she was in the audience almost every week.

The camera operators knew exactly where each contestant's fans were seated that week. When Ryan introduced a performance, the director could cut to an audience shot of supporters holding up signs. My cousins visited and made signs, and I had random fans who brought signs too.

My supporters called themselves the Philnatics, and I still hear from the leader of the group. They started a website and even posted a song that I'd written in college. Some Christian radio stations around the country even played the song, though I had no idea how they got ahold of it. I'm guessing it was through my father-in-law, Mark, because he was plugged in to the Philnatics. (He told me he'd always be my biggest supporter, and he's a man of his word.) My fans set up online discussion boards and created tribute videos. Wherever we went on the *American Idol* tour, I met new Philnatics.

Once you're established on *Idol*, the schedule gets busier. When the live performances began, the show started scheduling interviews with news outlets around the country. They woke you at a crazy early hour, sat you in front of a monitor in a room that was completely dark except for a light shining in your face, and patched you through to reporters from all over the country for a bunch of television interviews.

Imagine that it's 3:00 a.m. in Los Angeles, and you've been awakened for a live interview with a 6:00 a.m. morning news show in Florida. This goes on all day, all week, with all of the *Idol* contestants. It was crazy how many interviews we did. And we're not talking about just the big television markets. I promoted the show on programs in cities I'd never heard of.

In addition to the packed promotional schedule, we had to make time to shop for clothes to wear onstage. It was incredible—you'd walk into some stores and they'd say, "Please wear this. You can have it." The store employees knew who we were at this point. They worked in Hollywood, after all, so the show's stylists only had to let them know that the *American Idol* people would be coming in. Aldo, a company that manufactures footwear, told us we could have a free pair of boots every week, and plenty of other companies sent us clothing too. During the semifinals, our individual weekly clothing budget was $500.

We went shopping with the stylists and then rehearsed with the band. More interviews, more rehearsing, and then another live show. Sing your song for the judges. Lather, rinse, repeat.

I still felt self-conscious whenever the camera was on me. My second song of the semifinals was "Missing You" by John

Waite, and I nailed it. It was maybe my favorite performance. Some people said they preferred one of my other songs, but when I watch the shows now, "Missing You" is the one I like the most.

As if the pressure wasn't excruciating enough already, you could always make it worse by visiting DialIdol.com, a website that tracked *American Idol* voting trends. By measuring telephone busy signals, the site predicted which contestants were in danger of elimination each week. If you were one of the bottom three vote-getters that week according to DialIdol, you had reason to sweat. The website's predictions weren't always right, but it was rare to see someone eliminated who wasn't in the bottom three of its list.

There are some people who say that the *American Idol* results are rigged, that the producers choose the winners. That was not my experience. In my experience, AT&T counted the votes, AT&T submitted the results, and Ryan Seacrest announced them.

After I performed "Missing You," DialIdol.com listed me as one of the top vote-getters that week. Four other contestants were sent home, which meant I'd made it to the top sixteen. Week three of the semifinals, however, was not so great. First of all, I sang poorly that night, and DialIdol.com listed me as one of the bottom vote-getters. Second, my friend Sundance, a guy with a really beautiful voice, was eliminated before the finals.

I survived somehow, and that's when life really changed. Up until that point, the show merely covered our expenses, but when the finals began, we started getting paid like an actor on a series. For the first few weeks we could all walk around the mall and nobody noticed. Once we made it to the top twelve, however, people started taking photos and wanting autographs.

Some of us tried to attend church the following Sunday—it was Jordin Sparks, Melinda Doolittle, and me, and I think Chris Sligh was there as well. We walked into a church during the first song. Unfortunately, we were a big distraction. People left the pews to be near us; people asked us to sign their Bibles in the middle of the service. And this was in LA, where folks are used to seeing famous celebrities all the time.

When the top ten finalists appeared on the cover of *People* magazine, I had a little bit of stubble on my face. That photo earned me a call from the chief of naval operations: "Son, you better shave your face," he said. "You are the most famous sailor in the world right now, and you need to look like a sailor." At this point I was officially assigned to the Navy's Los Angeles recruiting district, yet that office never contacted me, never talked to me, never did anything. They just sent some people to one of the shows.

As if things weren't hectic enough, my Navy bandleader in Jacksonville was trying to check up on me. I'll admit that it was hard to reach me, so when he finally did, he was upset. "You need to be on call to me at all times," he yelled. "I need to know where you are."

I didn't mean to sound disrespectful, but I told him, "Sir, I just got off the phone with the chief of naval operations."

Other than Kendra and the Navy, the only people who had access to my new phone worked for *American Idol*. When I first met one of the *Idol* security officers, he introduced himself as a member of the "wife patrol." When you're messing around with other girls, he explained, it was his job to distract your wife or girlfriend. I was taken aback. These were the guys running "security" for *American Idol*?

"Is that really a thing?" I asked.

"Yes," he replied, "that's a thing."

"Well," I said, "I'm not going to need that."

It was true—I didn't need the wife patrol. At least not yet.

Other than Chris Sligh, I was the only other married contestant among the twelve finalists. During the finals I roomed with Chris, Blake Lewis, and Chris Richardson. The four of us had an apartment together, and the guys allowed me to share a room with Kendra. We snuck her in late at night. We were together, but we weren't alone, since we always had either Chloe or McKayla in the room with us.

It was tough to maintain a consistent spiritual life when your whole existence revolved around your participation in a nationally televised singing competition. Some of the other finalists—probably half of us—were believers, and several of us started doing devotions together. Jordin Sparks's pastor back in Arizona sent us some devotions, and we also gathered to sing praise songs.

Our little group began to feel like a family. We were all experiencing an extremely intense situation—we were all in the other dimension, and we were all in it together. We understood each other in a way that no one else could.

Week after week, I kept making it to the next round. But I never unpacked my bags at the apartment; I didn't know how long I'd be there. The money we all received when we made it to the top twelve made me feel rich, however, and Kendra and I paid off debts, including the cost of our plane tickets. All the contestants earned an additional paycheck per episode after that. The finals consisted of two episodes per week: Tuesday night we performed; Wednesday night was the elimination show.

With fewer singers remaining, our performances became longer. The top twelve had less than two minutes per song, but every week we were given a little more time. Each contestant was assigned a vocal coach, either Dorian Holley or Debra Byrd, who helped us choose a key for our songs and edit them to the time allotted. I usually tried to sing my songs in the original key, but the coaches offered suggestions and helped with the arrangement.

A typical week went something like this: Wednesday night after the elimination episode we went out to dinner together; it was essentially a send-off party for the people sent home. In the finals, it's just one person per week. By Thursday morning it was back to work, as we learned the musical theme for the next week's show. We had a list of songs to choose from, and we each met with one of the vocal coaches and the associate music director to select our song and work on the arrangement. Every contestant recorded a rough version of the song for the show's bandleader and music director to reference when scoring the final arrangement.

I've worked with many good musicians, but I'm convinced that *American Idol* has one of the best bands in the world. They learned and flawlessly performed a batch of new songs every single week. For example, the band included Paul Jackson Jr. on guitar, who played on Michael Jackson's "Thriller." When these musicians weren't playing on *Idol*, they were on the road with major artists (Usher, for example) who only hire the best.

Fridays were studio days, when we'd record our song. The show first offered these recordings for sale on the *Idol* website as digital downloads, then later on iTunes.

American Idol introduced a new wrinkle with season six: celebrity mentors. When it came time to pick a song for the week, they told us the musical theme and who the mentors would be. For example, "This week the theme is British Invasion music, your mentors will be Peter Noone and Lulu, and here's a list of songs." By the time you met each mentor, you'd already rehearsed the song for that week's show.

The mentoring sessions took place on Saturday, and it honestly wasn't really much of a mentorship; it was more of a filming opportunity. We had maybe thirty minutes with a mentor, if that, and the producers didn't always prepare us well. With Diana Ross, for example, we were given a strong lecture beforehand: *Don't make eye contact with her. Don't reach out to shake her hand. Don't hug her. Refer to her as Ms. Ross. She's a major diva; treat her as such.*

When I actually met her on the set, she gave me a big hug, cheek to cheek, and said, "Oh my gosh, it has been such fun watching your journey." She asked me questions: "How old is your baby now? When was she born?" I wasn't supposed to make eye contact with her, but *she* was making eye contact with me!

With Diana Ross, the song choices included her solo material and selections from her work with the Supremes. When the theme was British Invasion, Peter Noone from Herman's Hermits worked with the guys and Scottish singer Lulu worked with the girls. Other weeks it was Gwen Stefani, Tony Bennett, Jennifer Lopez, Martina McBride, Jon Bon Jovi, and Barry Gibb. Every week we were able to hang out with famous artists.

We performed the shortened version of our song for the mentor, who told us what we could do to improve it. Other times we might just get an assessment. If you were fortunate like me, you might have the chance to sing a song for Diana Ross that the legendary Marvin Gaye once sang. He was a lifetime influence of mine, somebody whose music I snuck into the house as a kid.

I wasn't allowed to listen to "Let's Get It On" when I was young. My older brother and I each had Walkmans, and Keith snuck the music of hair metal bands into the house while I snuck in Marvin Gaye songs and that kind of music.

Gaye was a brilliant singer/songwriter, and his soulful voice made me want to hear more. Because of *American Idol*, I was able to meet Diana Ross, an R&B icon who recorded duets with Marvin Gaye!

At that point I was letting one of the producers choose my songs because I didn't know many on the list. I didn't know much of the Supremes music, so the producer suggested "I'm Going to Make You Love Me." When I had trouble selecting something during British Invasion week, he chose "Tobacco Road." Top ten week was Gwen Stefani and her influences, and he recommended "Every Breath You Take" by The Police.

Everyone who watches *Idol* has heard the judges say, "That was a poor song choice." The reality is that we didn't have complete freedom in selecting our own songs. We didn't have an unlimited list to choose from, and whoever was first to choose that week might pick the song I wanted. If you had last choice, you ended up with whatever was left.

When I sang "Blaze of Glory" during Bon Jovi week, it was one of the only songs left on the list. I loved that song, but I didn't know it as well as "Living on a Prayer" and "You Give Love a Bad Name." It was the producer who said, "Hey man, try this 'Blaze of Glory' song." I ended up lowering the key by about three steps, or, at least, I tried to. Jon Bon Jovi made me hit all the high notes when he was mentoring me. Still he was great. All of them were.

Honestly, I didn't have a single bad experience with any of the mentors. Gwen Stefani was amazing. I was a little surprised when her first comment was, "Wow, I didn't think you'd be that good," but I was thrilled to hear that she thought I was good! She was super sweet, and she brought gifts for my wife. "Hey, I know what it's like to be an entertainment spouse," she told me. "Your wife may feel completely forgotten right now, and I just want to give you something for her."

After the mentoring sessions, the rest of the weekend might consist of more interviews, photo shoots, filming a commercial as a group, or choosing stage clothes for the live performance. Once you're in the finals, the weekly clothing allowance increases, and that's not counting the free pair of Aldo boots.

Regarding my wardrobe, I had one especially bad performance after the live shows began. It was a *really* bad night. I sang "I Need You" by LeAnn Rimes, and I looked like an idiot. I'd never worked with this particular stylist before, and he had me wear a hat that pushed one of my ears down. They put hats on me so I wouldn't look like Chris Daughtry. I'm not a hat guy, but on the show I wore a hat almost every week. We weren't required to listen to the stylist, but I had to trust people at that point because I'd never been on television. I had no confidence in myself because I was thinking, *I'm twenty-eight years old, and I'm not a star. I obviously don't know what I'm doing.*

I was listening to everybody's advice, but you could tell that it wasn't right for me that night. I wore an olive shirt that emphasized my pale skin, my ear was folded over, and the moment I started singing I sounded terrible. Simon Cowell really ripped hard into me that night on camera. "Phil, I didn't get that at all," he said. "I thought the hat, the big eyes, it was just insane."

I agreed with him on the hat, but the comment about my eyes? What was I supposed to do? Did he want me to squint? And yet, after the show was over, I walked out into the backstage hallway and Simon was standing there. "Hey, great job tonight, Phil," he said.

On camera Simon had blasted me, so, needless to say, I was confused.

"I should clarify," said Simon. "You were terrible, which gives me the opportunity to tell you how terrible you did, and that boosts the ratings. So, great job tonight. Way to take one for the team."

He was funny like that, which made it hard to be upset with him. Simon could be absolutely brutal on the show, but he was still a decent guy. He'd see my daughter Chloe backstage and give her presents and high fives. He once gave her a stuffed cow and she named it Simon the Cow.

Mondays were rehearsal days, this time with the house band. It was the final opportunity to make any last-minute changes to the song's arrangement. Tuesday was the dress rehearsal, and later the live performance in front of the judges and everyone watching at home. That evening, America voted on who stayed and who went home.

Wednesday night was the elimination show, and then the entire process started again.

I've compared competing on *American Idol* to living in an alternate reality. In this alternate reality, I was heavily insulated from my church life. After a few weeks, it was as if I no longer *remembered* church.

If my church didn't like me singing "Tobacco Road," why should I care? I was living the dream, performing on television in front of millions. *They'll live.*

I didn't know it when I was on the show, but ministers from all over the country were sending me letters of disapproval. They sent them to Florida and Hollywood. They sent messages via social media. (The show didn't give me all this "fan mail" until after I was eliminated.)

The *American Idol* experience was an emotionally crazy time. I remember being at the home of a huge pop star, hanging out in the piano room with about a dozen other people. A famous actress was in the room and sat on the piano bench next to me, getting drunk. This woman is an A-list celebrity, and I was at the piano, playing some of the Christian songs I'd written. People started leaving the room, until just the two of us were left. I figured it was time for me to leave too, but she said, "No, keep playing. This is the first peace I've felt all year." So I just kept playing.

One night the *Idol* contestants were at a late-night LA party. I was sitting on one side of a couch and Melinda Doolittle was at the other end; in between us was one of the most successful songwriters in history. It was about two o'clock in the morning, and Melinda started talking about how tired she was. "I think I'm going to go get some Coke," she said. The songwriter immediately spoke up: "Oh honey, I've got some right here."

Melinda, of course, was talking about Coca-Cola, not cocaine. She is super shy—one of the sweetest, most innocent girls you'll ever meet. Melinda shook her head and told him, "That's okay." That was the world we were living in; a really different world.

This sort of interaction might have surprised me back in Jacksonville, but it was fairly typical in the world of *American Idol.* We were surrounded by television stars. It was fun meeting people I'd heard on the radio or seen on television, like Tiffani Amber Thiessen. She worked with the Make-A-Wish Foundation, so she wanted to befriend people from *American Idol.* Turns out that there were a lot of kids whose biggest wish was to meet the contestants, so I worked with her to make that happen.

When Paula Abdul found out about it, she started bringing gifts. Actually, she was already giving weekly presents to all the contestants, but when she heard the Make-A-Wish kids were coming, she started bringing even more gifts. She wanted to meet them.

We had wonderful experiences with celebrities, and we had bad experiences with celebrities. We read about ourselves in the news. I didn't know who I was anymore. As I chose my songs, I was thinking, *I've been a Christian my whole life and I've always loved the Lord. I went to a Christian college. I was a minister before coming here, and all of a sudden I don't know if I want to be a Christian singer. Maybe I want to be a secular singer.*

At the same time I had these thoughts, the finalists were also visiting LA clubs. We were expected to do this for publicity purposes, and there were drugs everywhere. Those who weren't doing drugs were almost always drinking. What confused me was that most of these Hollywood people were genuinely nice. I was in these clubs where folks were doing drugs and being sexually promiscuous, but at the same time they were caring people and fun to be around. A lot of them were more loving than some of the people I knew at church. *What do I do with that?*

I can't speak for everyone, but I think many of the other believers on the show were in some sort of spiritual crisis by the end of the season. In terms of what makes it on the air, *Idol* is a rather wholesome show, but the truth is that for those of us who make it on the show, it's a deep opportunity for self-discovery of the good, the bad, and the ugly.

CHAPTER 11

EVERYONE'S A CRITIC

EVERY WEEK AMERICA VOTED. Every week the experience was stressful. And every week I kept advancing. Once the finals began, Ryan Seacrest would announce on TV which singers were in the bottom two or three in terms of the voting, and I was in that bottom group almost every week. I can't say for sure, but I think I might have the record for number of appearances at the bottom.

Each time it happened, I said to myself, *Okay, I'm ready! I'm ready to go!* My daughter Chloe told me on the phone how much she missed her daddy, and I always said, "Oh baby, I miss you too."

Keep in mind that my daughters spent a lot of time living

with Kendra's parents, and my in-laws had them pray nightly for Daddy. "I prayed that you will come home," Chloe told me, and it touched my heart. Whenever Ryan announced that I was one of the bottom vote-getters, I was okay with it. Daddy would finally come home.

But not yet.

It was sad to see my fellow contestants eliminated. Chris Sligh went home after one particular performance during the top ten week. He was a good singer, but the song he chose had a very tricky rhythm and his timing was off. Plenty of viewers liked him, but they didn't vote for him that time. Chris was so convinced his time on *American Idol* was up that he was willing to wager on being the bottom vote-getter that week. Sure enough, as he hugged everyone during his post-elimination song, Chris said to me on-air, "You owe me fifty bucks."

Chris's departure was followed by Gina Glocksen and Haley Scarnato. In each of those weeks, I was right there with them at the bottom, but my name was never called.

Top seven week was a country music theme. I sang "Where the Blacktop Ends" by Keith Urban. That's when the judges said I'd at last found my genre, my musical identity.

But it wasn't me. I was in a Navy rock band, singing Led Zeppelin and Guns N' Roses. That was my life. I was a rocker then, and I'm still a rocker. When I sing praise and worship music, it's rocking praise and worship music.

So why didn't I embrace that rock music persona on the show? The biggest reason was Chris Daughtry. We were both white guys with shaved heads, so there was already somewhat of a physical resemblance. More important, Daughtry had filled the role of the rock guy in the previous season, so there was no way I could experience success in the same niche. I would look like a copycat, an imitator. I had to occupy a different world, but by this time I didn't even know what world I lived in. I couldn't tell you. The judges decided that country music was my thing, but I wasn't totally convinced.

Sanjaya was eliminated during country week. Despite what everyone read about him in the press, Sanjaya was a better singer than most people realized. He was a shy, cute kid with a big smile—a contagious smile. The implication was that a bunch of young female fans were keeping him alive on the show, an implication that the producers fed into by repeatedly showing a girl in the audience who wept whenever he sang.

I thought Sanjaya did a good job of remaining calm. He never, ever let the negative coverage upset him. He was asked by reporters, "Do you think you deserve to be on the show? Do you think you should be here when there are better singers out there?" It never weighed on him. There wasn't a single moment when Sanjaya said to me "I'm sad" or "I'm depressed." He was an upbeat teenager. He was a cheery kid, and I was rooting for him.

He has a great voice, and I think what people saw on TV was a kid who'd never performed outside of school productions. He didn't grow up singing in church like many of the other contestants, and suddenly he was on a soundstage in front of millions. When I was on *American Idol*, there were no monitors to help you hear yourself sing onstage. I'd performed numerous concerts with the Navy band, so I'd learned how to adjust when my monitors weren't working. Sanjaya had not. I was sad when he was eliminated. His presence would be missed.

———

Idol was one giant roller-coaster ride, or at least it was for me. Some days I had so much fun. One day we were able to spend time with legendary music producer Quincy Jones. We talked to him about working with Michael Jackson, about the making of *Thriller*, and about recording songs like "Billie Jean." On another day I talked with Bon Jovi, who was one of the coolest people I'd ever met. And we all received gifts from celebrities like Jennifer Lopez and Carrie Underwood, who brought us jewelry from Tiffany & Co.

The live performances, however, were not so much fun. I'd sit backstage beforehand and sing "Hold Me Jesus" just to calm my nerves. Sometimes Jordin and Melinda would sit down and sing it with me. They did that a few times, because those moments before we went to face the judges were such a nerve-wracking time.

Jordin received plenty of positive feedback from the judges. Blake Lewis earned great comments too. But me? Every week was different. Unpredictable. One week the judges loved me and the next week I heard, "You stink."

My mom was mortified whenever Simon would say something negative to me. Sometimes she cried. Every time anybody said or wrote anything negative about me, she took it as a personal attack.

"Is Simon Cowell really that mean?" is often the first question people ask me. And the answer is yes—he *really is* that mean. But he's also hilarious. He's more of a comedian than anything else, but that's only true if you can handle the heat. If not, as the saying goes, then you'd better stay out of the kitchen. I couldn't always make out what Simon was saying because it was difficult to hear the judges when standing on the *American Idol* stage. Depending on the audience's reaction, we knew when he was saying something harsh. When the audience cheered, we figured it was something good.

There were contestants who thought Simon picked on them quite a bit. Haley Scarnato was irritated by the fact that he commented on her legs, because she liked to wear shorts. There were plenty of things about Simon that bothered each contestant, but remember that everybody was okay enough with him to audition for the show. We all knew what we were getting into.

I was dealing with plenty of my own issues, but Simon's negativity wasn't one of them. By the time I made it on the show I was fairly desensitized to criticism. I'd already dealt with that older gentleman back in Wichita who told me what I'd done wrong almost every time I sang in church. And it wasn't much easier for me at college. Dr. Mauldin had a reputation for being a bit intimidating, but it's because he pushed us. And he pushed us because he believed in us. And sometimes that was scary. Like the first time I sang a solo in the Lee Singers. He ended his critique with, "You'll be lucky if I ever give you a solo again."

What's crazy is that I wasn't planning to sing a solo that day. We were performing at a church on Sunday morning, and Dr. Mauldin introduced a song that featured one of the other guys in my section. Dr. Mauldin didn't realize the other guy wasn't there until the song started, so he looked at me and said, "You sing it."

Trouble was, I didn't know the words. My voice cracked. Honestly, I did a terrible job. But a Lee Singer is supposed to be prepared at all times. Dr. Mauldin would sometimes call out new people and have them sing a number they'd never rehearsed because you were expected to know all the music in the folder. He expected a level of excellence that I grew to appreciate.

Later that same day, on Sunday evening, we performed the song again, and Dr. Mauldin once again had me sing the solo. By then I'd learned it. I did well, and the following week I was assigned my own solo.

It took somebody like Dr. Mauldin, who was willing to be tough on me, to make me better. It was a similar scenario in the Navy. In the military you're expected to do a job, and if you don't do it right, you hear about it. So by the time I met Simon Cowell, I'd been through what felt like a lifetime of brutal feedback. It didn't affect me the same way anymore.

Paula and Randy had supported me consistently throughout the season. That meant a lot to me because I had been a big fan of Paula Abdul, and Randy is a gifted music producer. You can imagine what a huge compliment it was to me when he said my voice reminded him of Steve Perry from Journey.

Randy recorded and toured with Journey in the 1980s, and he once asked me offstage, "Did you listen to a lot of Journey growing up?" He started telling me about life on the road with them. He compared me to Steve Perry, but Steve is a legend in rock music and has an incredible vocal range. Journey was one of the bands we covered when I was in the Navy band, and I felt incredibly honored that Randy would even mention me in the same breath as Steve.

I thought I wanted that rock star life when I was younger—touring the world, performing in front of thousands every night. Back in high school, all of my friends—both girls and guys—would write in my yearbook or on the back of the senior photos they gave me: "You're going to be famous someday. I can't wait to come to one of your concerts." My whole life I thought that's what I wanted, but it was during *American Idol* when I realized the rock star life wasn't for me.

Despite being on television, I was still essentially a nobody. I didn't have a hit record, my songs weren't on the radio—but *Idol* alone was enough to alter my daily life. One time Blake and Sanjaya and I were in the Apple store in an

LA shopping mall when some kids spotted us and started screaming. Sanjaya in particular was getting a lot of press coverage at the time, and that moment was like one of those Beatles scenes from the 1960s. Kids were running after us, just going nuts. They ended up chasing us out of the mall, and I remember thinking, *I'm not ready for this.*

After Chris Sligh was eliminated, Kendra essentially moved into the apartment. She was already staying in my room at night, but we still had to keep sneaking her in. *American Idol* wasn't family friendly. One night security showed up at the apartment at 2:00 a.m. (They had their own key, so they could walk in at any time.) My sister was visiting me at the time, but when they opened the door and saw me with another woman— one they didn't recognize—they just said, "Oh, sorry, Phil."

Kendra had a reserved seat in the audience every week, but even when she was holding the baby they wouldn't let her into the studio before the rest of the audience. A couple of times it was raining, and they wouldn't let Kendra take shelter; she had to wait outside with our daughter. I fought for my family, but nothing changed. After a while we just stopped fighting.

The show's producers did a decent job of portraying life as a contestant on *American Idol*. We had a packed schedule almost every day, yet no two days were exactly the same. Every morning, a car picked us up from the apartment; most weekdays we headed for the TV studio, and on weekends we had the mentor meetings and a Ford car commercial. Every Sunday we shot a new commercial, and some of them were rather elaborate.

Somewhere in there we had to fit in all the photo shoots—so many shoots! They were especially draining for me. Many of the girls loved them because the producers always provided professional hair styling and makeup. They also brought in huge wardrobes full of clothes, and you were able to keep whatever you chose to put on.

But the producers didn't show everything. Just as our TV audience had to wait each week for a new episode, the contestants had our fair share of waiting. Whenever we met with the mentors or went shopping, there were long periods of sitting and waiting. Sometimes we waited together, other times alone. We waited at the production studios too. The *American Idol* studio was across the hall from the *Dancing with the Stars* studio, so *Dancing* contestant Billy Ray Cyrus would sometimes wander over and talk to the *Idol* people while we waited for the next thing to happen.

Something most home viewers don't know is that the "live" performances from the guest artists were not really live. When Fergie performed on *Idol*, it was presented as live, but she actually sang her song several times and the producers selected the best take. In fact, there were three stand-in models for Simon, Randy, and Paula who wore wigs and sat in their seats. The director made sure to capture the audience shots from behind so no one at home was the wiser.

All of our performances in front of the judges were live, of course, but the recap videos you saw at the end of each show were typically taken from our sound check recorded earlier in the day. One time I sang well in my sound check but terribly in my live performance. During the recap it showed me killing the song. I wished nobody had seen my live performance.

I'm convinced that the judges sometimes watched our sound check performances from their dressing rooms. I say that because I remember Paula commenting on something that wasn't part of the live performance, and it reminded me that the judges could see those dress rehearsals.

There were plenty of mundane or unbecoming activities that the *American Idol* producers never showed. They didn't film all of the behind-the-scenes routines. They were never at our apartment or the recording sessions, and they never followed us at the mall. It was only when we arrived at the *Idol* studios that they turned the cameras on. For example, many contestants received cortisone shots for their vocal cords. This sort of thing is common for singers, because steroids help tired vocal cords work better, but who wants to see that? The truth is that we were exhausted from all the early mornings and late nights.

Sure, the hours were long, but no one wants to hear complaints from a guy who was paid to sing on television every week. It's true that we were living the good life. We ate catered meals prepared by professional chefs. We had security guards whenever we went out in public. We were hanging out with some of the music industry's biggest stars.

Thanks to *Idol*, I learned more about the humanity of

celebrities than I ever imagined. When you're surrounded by famous people, you see that their lives are like everyone else's. They may own fancy cars, but they drive to work just like you do. They live in expensive houses, but every night they crawl into bed just like you do. And they have just as many insecurities—maybe even worse insecurities—because they face constant pressure to succeed.

While the *American Idol* set was generally wholesome, the moment you stepped outside the television studio was when everything broke loose. I experienced it all, from women handing me nude pictures with their phone numbers to being offered drugs at a party and free drinks at every club I walked into. I didn't hit the clubs as much as some others because my family was in town, but going out at night was considered another chance to gain publicity for the show. If a camera crew or photographer was there, it helped your name stay in the public eye.

Having seen my fair share of stars at the LA clubs, I won't deny that we witnessed some real drug and alcohol problems. That trend has been well-documented, at least among younger celebrities, and we saw it firsthand. The good news is that I rarely saw my fellow *Idol* contestants doing drugs or drinking a lot.

Like Sanjaya, Jordin Sparks was also a minor during the competition, so her mother or grandmother was with her at all times. Jordin's story is a great case study in perseverance. Contestants are allowed to audition as many times as they want, and Jordin had to audition twice during season six—first in Phoenix, then again in Seattle—before she received her golden ticket. It's hard to imagine that, because Jordin is an incredible singer.

———

I can't tell you how many jackets and pairs of shoes I own thanks to *American Idol*. For example, during Bon Jovi week I was given a couple of his jackets. These were designer leather coats that typically cost between $5,000 and $10,000 apiece, some really sweet biker jackets. I wore one of them during my performance of "Blaze of Glory," then another one for the next night's elimination episode. He'd previously worn both of them. They weren't a perfect fit because Bon Jovi is a big guy—strong and stocky—and back then I was still pretty skinny.

I connected with Bon Jovi on a different level than any of the other mentors. I wasn't starstruck when I met him, but I was honored to be in the same room. I thought it was cool because Keith used to sneak Bon Jovi music into the house when we were kids. In fact, my father once caught my brother listening to "Living on a Prayer," and Keith tried to convince him that it was a Christian song. That made my dad laugh. He was very strict, but at the same time, he was supportive. He just didn't want us listening to music that would influence us negatively. Keith wasn't in big trouble, but Dad did throw away the tape.

During my mentoring session, Bon Jovi was extremely kind and complimentary. After I sang for him, he said,

"Whoa, man, that was awesome." Later my parents said, "We've always loved Bon Jovi." No, you didn't!

Growing up, my family listened to gospel artists like Sandi Patty and Carman. Their music was considered acceptable. On road trips we could play tapes of contemporary Christian groups like Petra, but only if we wore headphones. We didn't play them on the car stereo because they were rock and roll. What's funny is that my mom loved the oldies and my dad loved jazz, and jazz is not Christian music at all. It's one of the most drug-influenced musical genres, and many of those old-school jazz legends died of drug overdoses.

MTV was also forbidden in our house except for when Michael Jackson's videos were on, because my mom loved the Jackson 5 growing up. She would switch the channel to MTV every now and then, just to see if "Thriller" was playing. Even though that particular video included a disclaimer about the occult imagery, it was the one music video we were allowed to watch. This was before Michael Jackson began behaving erratically; my mother thought he was cool in part because they were both born on August 29.

All that was in the 1980s. As we grew older, our parents became more lenient. By the 1990s we were openly listening to Guns N' Roses, Aerosmith, Mariah Carey, Whitney Houston, and Boyz II Men. After all, it's much easier to keep a ten-year-old from listening to certain music than a sixteen-year-old. Also, the more freedom my older brother had, the more freedom I had, since it's tough to have a different set of rules for each child.

My exposure to various musical genres was helpful during my time on *American Idol* because the game had changed over the first five seasons. When it first debuted, *Idol* was basically a karaoke competition. In the first season, the contestants didn't even perform with a band—they sang along to pre-recorded soundtracks. By season five, not only did they have a live band, but Chris Daughtry started shaping the music to his own personal style. While most contestants sang their songs exactly like the artists who recorded them, Daughtry performed powerful rock versions instead of watered-down pop tracks. His attitude was *I'm going to do this song, but I'm not going to do it like everyone else. I'm going to do it like me.*

In many ways, season five reshaped everybody's expectations. That group of finalists—Taylor Hicks, Katherine McPhee, Elliott Yamin, Chris Daughtry, Paris Bennett, Kellie Pickler, Ace Young, Bucky Covington, Mandisa, Lisa Tucker—all went on to have singing careers. Every one of them. Some people dogged Taylor Hicks, but that dude is still touring. He has a platinum-selling record. He's done well. Remember what he was doing before *Idol*: singing in local party bands.

The early seasons of *American Idol* featured quite a few "normal" people in the top ten—people who didn't go on to become stars. But all the finalists in season five went on to Broadway or recording contracts or whatever, so everyone figured that the following season would introduce another special group of singers. But it was just us. I can't speak for everybody, but several of the season six contestants felt like we didn't deserve to be there. It might have been a better season if we'd been more competitive, more assertive—if we displayed our individual artistic personas a bit more.

By the time *Idol* started season six, the show expected more originality from everybody, but Blake Lewis was the only one who delivered. Blake had more experience than the rest of us combined at remixing songs. His versions would irritate some of the mentors; for example, Bon Jovi seemed uncomfortable with Blake's arrangement of "You Give Love a Bad Name," and he definitely made his feelings known. Yet that week was perhaps Blake's biggest performance. The rest of us thought, *Blake's going down this week*, because he radically changed Bon Jovi's song, but that was the night when Blake became the one to beat. He played the game very, very well even though he wasn't an extremely competitive person. By the time the season was ending, Blake's attitude had changed to *I'm done with this experience. I'm ready to get on with my recording career.*

There was just something about Blake's star power. The guy didn't consider himself as much of a singer—he was more comfortable beat-boxing or producing and remixing. Don't get me wrong; he was a good singer who stayed on pitch. We were all good karaoke singers, but the audience went nuts for Blake. He changed the game moving forward, because in the following seasons, if you didn't have a star persona, if you didn't have an identity, you probably didn't make it to the finals.

CHAPTER 12

"IT'S NOT ABOUT YOU"

BY 2007, *Idol* was probably the most popular television show on the planet. The producers knew they were operating a cultural phenomenon, and they wanted to do something positive with it. They decided to create a special week called "Idol Gives Back"—a charitable campaign and fundraiser for people living in poverty, both in America and Africa. Some of the donations, for example, went to people impacted by Hurricane Katrina.

"Idol Gives Back" took place during top six week, and we all sang inspirational songs. I chose "The Change" by Garth Brooks. The elimination show featured an all-star cast, which made it feel more impressive than even the season finale. We had the honor of singing a brand-new song composed by "We Are the World" producer Quincy Jones. The list of special guest performers was incredible and included Earth, Wind, and Fire; Carrie Underwood; Rascal Flatts; Josh Groban; Kelly Clarkson; Fergie; Green Day; and Annie Lennox. Celine Dion sang "If I Can Dream" as a duet with Elvis Presley by using vintage footage of Elvis. I was blown away. They somehow made it look like Elvis was standing right next to her onstage. The remaining finalists joined Celine and Elvis to finish the performance. I don't know how they pulled it off from a technical standpoint, but the six of us sang along with them.

At the end of the elimination show, Ryan Seacrest made it seem like Jordin was on the chopping block, only to announce that everyone was safe after all. "How could we let anybody go on a charity night?" he said. This meant that the fan votes would continue to add up, with the bottom two contestants going home the following week.

Thank goodness Kendra had already talked to me about my fears. "You're sending the message to your brain that this is about you," she said. "The reason you're nervous is because you're prideful. You're worried about the way people are going to perceive you. You're worried about the way you're going to look.

"There are a million great singers in the United States, but you're here for some reason. God has appointed you to be here. Because of that, it's about Him, no matter what. If you can lean on Him, He's going to give you the strength you need. It's not about you, and when you make it about you, it's not going to be as enjoyable an experience."

Every week, my wife was giving me Bible verses. She encouraged me, kept me focused. Kendra was so influential during that time because she was focused on the spiritual perspective, especially when I wasn't. "You're caught up in the world around you," she said, "but God is doing something special in your life."

She was absolutely right. All of a sudden it clicked in my brain. I didn't need to be nervous. That's the thing: If you're having one bad performance after another, it's not because you're just having a bad day; it's probably because you're not as good as everybody else. From that point forward, I decided to just get up onstage and enjoy the ride. Maybe God *was* doing something. Maybe this experience would lead to ministry opportunities down the road. You can see the change in my performances. You can see that a switch was flipped. Before, I was terrified; for several weeks I looked like a deer in the headlights. Suddenly, I was comfortable.

Kendra was the buffer between me and the outside world, fielding calls and requests from family and friends. When people came to visit, I was able to see them—but only briefly, and only after the show. We spent maybe an hour or two together, but that's it. I was secluded most of the time, and it needed to be that way because the people who know you want to tell you everything you're doing wrong. They want to tell you how you can win, how you can do better, and it only creates unnecessary pressure. The contestants were rarely allowed on the internet because the producers knew how many people blogged about *American Idol*. Yet we still found ways to get online and read about the show.

A website called VoteForTheWorst.com really took off during season six when they started encouraging *Idol* watchers to vote for Sanjaya. A site like that can make you lose confidence, because they were basically making fun of the show. But it led to one of the most significant transformational moments for me on *American Idol*: I went from being extremely self-conscious to not giving a rip what the critics said about me. I don't know exactly how that happened, but the change occurred around the same time Kendra convinced me that it wasn't all about me.

By the time I sang "Blaze of Glory" during top five week, I was completely comfortable. I felt good about my performance.

The next night was the elimination episode. Because the previous week was "Idol Gives Back," this time two contestants would be going home. Kendra was in the audience, as usual, next to a couple of sailors. I'd never met them before—I just called the naval base I was assigned to and told them, "Let's bring out some guys in uniform." I suspected that my elimination was imminent, so I thought the sailors might make it on camera and thus make the Navy happy.

When it came time for the first elimination, Ryan Seacrest asked Melinda, LaKisha, and me to join him center stage. He declared Melinda safe, which put me in the bottom two. As LaKisha and I waited on edge, Ryan did the standard reality TV pause. I'd been among the bottom vote-getters several times before, but this time I was not safe. This time I was the one going home.

I felt some strange emotions that night. I was relieved, because the pressure was finally gone. It had been a beautiful experience. They showed a video of my journey and I got a little emotional. Then it was time for my last song. I've always thought that it was fitting to sing "Blaze of Glory" again as I was leaving—an appropriate song to go out on.

As I sang, I walked out into the audience to say goodbye. I hugged Randy and Paula and Simon, and I thanked each of them away from the microphone. Next I greeted the Navy guys in the audience. (At least that idea worked.) Finally, I got a hug and kiss from Kendra.

When I climbed back onstage for the final notes, LaKisha was wiping away tears, Jordin was bawling, Chris Richardson was crying, Blake Lewis looked sad, Melinda looked sad. I thought, *Isn't it funny that we're all sad when other people are eliminated?* They all stood up to meet me, and I smiled at them while I kept singing. It was emotional and bittersweet, but I had to finish the song because it was my last moment, and I didn't know if I would ever have another. I wanted my final performance to be one I was proud of. Melinda embraced me first, then it turned into one big group hug.

About twenty minutes later, Chris Richardson met the same fate. We both made it to the top five week, so—rightly or wrongly—I will always claim top five status. The show gave both of us the same bonus for being in the top five. We lasted the same number of weeks, and on a show like *American Idol*, a week means a lot.

After I finished singing, they took Chris and me to a room to meet with the show's psychologists. The contestants talked to them throughout the season, but those sessions were mostly informal. "How are you doing? How are you feeling about everything?" This time they had us sit down. A guy named Joe from 19 Entertainment also talked to us, saying, "Hey, we're excited about working with you guys. We're really excited about what the future holds."

Apparently Joe said that to all of the finalists. My guess is they were trying to help the contestants taper off from the fame of being on television. They don't want anyone to jump off a cliff after being eliminated. You can't control someone's mental stability, after all, and there is psychological trauma that can happen without you realizing it. Not just the trauma of being eliminated but of being on *American Idol* in the first place. Once I made it through the whole experience, I saw how pointless a lot of it was. I thought, *I've reached the pinnacle, and it's not that bright.*

In a way I'd achieved my musical dreams, yet realizing those dreams through *American Idol* had cheapened them a bit. I wasn't there based on my merit; I was there based on Simon Cowell's assessment or Randy Jackson's assessment or Paula Abdul's assessment of my merit. In many ways the show is all about the judges, and the rest of us are merely extras.

After the show was over, Simon shook my hand. "That was very classy, Chris," he said. "Great job. You really went out well."

I was grateful at first, but then I realized that Simon had just called me Chris. I went through nearly an entire season of *Idol*, yet I wondered at that moment if Simon ever really learned my name. *What a way to leave*, I thought.

Randy knew my name. I've seen Randy several times since *Idol*. I've heard from Paula a couple of times. She knew my name. I think Simon knew my name and just got mixed up. It still felt weird.

I think the psychologists wanted to give me an opportunity to breathe and reflect. They wanted me to release whatever I was feeling. If you're a crier, they want you to cry. If you're a talker, they want you to talk. But me? I stared straight ahead. Finally I said, "I'm okay. This isn't bad for me, this is good for me. I made it so much further than I thought I would."

Kendra was sitting next to me, holding my hand. "How are you doing?" she asked. Then she said to the psychologists, "He left on a good week. This was good. It's over. It's really, truly over now."

We thought it was over, but it wasn't.

The next day I was up again at 3:00 a.m. doing interviews with news outlets all over the country. Each time an *American Idol* finalist is eliminated, he or she is obligated to do the talk show circuit. Because we were eliminated the same week, I did some of these shows alongside Chris Richardson. For example, we appeared together on *The Ellen DeGeneres Show* and *The Tonight Show with Jay Leno* and MTV's *Total Request Live*.

As I traveled from studio to studio, from LA to New York, I was thinking, *Can I still get another opportunity out of this? Is this going to benefit my Navy career or hold me back?* The Navy had already told me that I wouldn't be allowed to participate in the *American Idol* tour. At first I was okay with it, since part of me was glad it was over and done. But the other part—the harder part for me to give up—was that the tour paid extremely well.

Think about it this way: The year before I'd made about $28,000 in the Navy. The *American Idol* tour, meanwhile, paid serious money. (It turned out to be even more when the tour added additional dates.) On top of that, each performer earned a percentage of the merchandise sales. But the Navy said I couldn't go.

The day of the *Ellen* taping, Kendra and I, along with McKayla, our youngest, were picked up in a limousine and escorted to Ellen DeGeneres's studio. Ellen greeted us in person. At this point I'd already met her a few times; she's good friends with Simon Fuller, the creator of *American Idol*, so she visited the show on occasion. (Ellen later went on to serve as a judge for one season.)

"Great job this year, Phil," she said. "I know this is a whirlwind, I know this is crazy, and I just want to give you and your wife some time together. I've had a meal catered for you, and then I have another surprise for you."

Ellen actually had one of the top chefs in Los Angeles prepare our meal. For what seemed like the first time in months, we had a chance to relax and exhale. The two dimensions we'd been living in became one. Kendra and I were together, and at the same time we were the guests of an Emmy Award–winning television host. After lunch, Ellen gave us a bunch of gifts.

In some ways Ellen was a Good Samaritan to me; she was someone who saw me bloodied and beaten and gave me rest. She knew I'd been pummeled by the newspapers and by Simon Cowell, but she didn't know about all the negative letters, or that I wasn't allowed to say goodbye to the congregation in Florida where I'd worked.

I should mention that the Navy had assigned a "handler" to travel with me during this media tour—I assume to make sure that I didn't say anything stupid—and she told Ellen's people that during the taping, Ellen was not allowed to ask me any questions about the *American Idol* tour, "because we're not letting Phil go."

Now, I don't have a recording of my appearance on the show, but I recall that one of the first things Ellen said to me on the set was something like, "Phil, what's this I hear about the Navy not letting you go on the *American Idol* tour?"

"Well," I replied, "I have a responsibility to the Navy. I think it's very generous that they allowed me to do *American Idol.*"

"What is your job in the Navy?" she asked.

"I'm a singer."

"Well, I think there's nothing better you could do with your voice than travel to arenas all over the country. They should let you go."

Right there she fought for me. My whole life I'd heard negative things about Ellen DeGeneres because she's openly liberal, but she fought for me. Around that time I'd finally received my "fan mail" from pastors disapproving of me. They criticized the songs I sang and the Hollywood culture, even the fact that the show's name included the word "Idol." They called me names. *You should leave the Church of God. You're not welcome here anymore.* Some even harassed my father. They wanted him to say publicly that he didn't approve of my *Idol* participation.

Meanwhile, Ellen supported me on national television. The Navy officer who traveled with me was frantic. She was going nuts backstage. Before my time on the show was over, Ellen asked me to perform. I sang "I Could Not Ask for More," and I walked off the set.

I could see my Navy handler on the phone, and I was pretty sure that Ellen's line of questioning might lead to a big

PR problem for the Navy. When she got off the phone, she said to me, "Congratulations, Phil. After this, we're going to have to let you go on the tour."

Ellen DeGeneres had just—indirectly—given me a big check. Isn't that crazy? I was excited about the opportunity to tour, but from a spiritual perspective, it was the worst thing that could have happened to me.

I briefly returned to Jacksonville, but my stay there was terrible. An officer met me with a toothbrush and told me to start scrubbing toilets. "You need to learn your place again," I was told. I had never washed a toilet to that point in my military career, but the Navy was clearly upset: "We let you go on *American Idol* because you were going to advertise the Navy, and you haven't worn your uniform once. You haven't done anything for the Navy."

What's funny is that in public they presented me with an award, and I did a couple of shows with the Navy rock band. (Only one member of the group was still mad at me; some were excited that I was on *American Idol*.) So in public I received a hero's welcome; in private I was cleaning toilets. In public I was cheered; in private I was told, "Be quiet and scrub." They wanted to remind me that while I might have made a name for myself in music, in the Navy I was still a nobody.

For every encouraging letter or email I received, I still had plenty of negative messages to digest. I definitely wasn't prepared for the critical feedback that had nothing to do with my musical abilities. *You are a shame to the church. How could you sing that song? How could you do this? You need to let the world know that you've abandoned Christ.*

I was devastated. I'd tried to maintain a proper spiritual perspective during my time on *Idol,* and now I was being attacked. Instead of pushing me closer to the Lord, the flood of rebukes and condemnation had the opposite effect. *I don't know how strong my faith is right now,* I thought.

CHAPTER 13

IDOL ON TOUR

———

SOON IT WAS TIME to head back to Los Angeles for the *American Idol* season finale. The top ten finalists also needed to start preparing for the *Idol* summer tour.

LaKisha was eliminated the week after Chris and I were, which meant that the show was down to Melinda, Jordin, and Blake. I'm pretty sure Simon thought Melinda was going to win, because Jordin was a bit of a sleeper. Jordin was consistently good, but she mostly played it safe until the final rounds. That's when she really opened up and started dominating.

By the time I was eliminated, I thought Jordin might be on her way to winning. Before that, I thought it was Melinda.

But who was I to say? Sanjaya could have won it for all I knew. Before he went home, everybody loved him. You should have seen the crowds; they all had signs for Sanjaya. There were plenty of cheers for all of the contestants, but the fans went absolutely *crazy* for Sanjaya.

Because I was part of the final show, I had to be there for the rehearsals. We learned new arrangements. We recorded new songs. We recorded new videos. We performed in the grand finale. All the finalists participated in the last show, along with winners from previous seasons and a host of special guest performers, including Tony Bennett, Gladys Knight, Bette Midler, Smokey Robinson, and BeBe & CeCe Winans (for whom Melinda Doolittle used to sing backup).

Melinda was eliminated in the top three week, a big surprise to those who thought she was going to win it all. It was down to Blake and Jordin. At one point before the finale, Blake suggested during an interview that fans should vote for Jordin. I'm not sure why, but he said stuff like "I just think she'd be a great American Idol."

Even if some of Blake's fans did switch their votes, Jordin absolutely deserved to win. Early on she sang songs that were less challenging and more in her comfort zone, but at the end she opened up and showed that her range was much larger than people thought. That's how I think she ran away with it.

I was glad to be part of such a spectacular event, and I was happy for Jordin, very proud of her. But now it was time to focus on *my* future.

Jordin Sparks was friends with Chaz Corzine, who's managed Christian artists including Amy Grant and Michael W. Smith. She introduced me to him. By now I knew that I was joining the *American Idol* tour, and that same week I learned that Chaz wanted to manage my career. I told the people from 19 Entertainment, "I'd prefer to be managed by these guys." They were cool with it and happy for me.

I started meeting with people in Nashville, Los Angeles, and New York, talking about potential record deals. Of course, there was one lingering problem: I was still a member of the United States Navy.

I originally enlisted for five years, but the last year was optional—a bonus year. The Navy gave me an extra $8,000 for it when I signed up, but if I repaid that bonus money, I'd be out in four years instead of five. Season six of *Idol* ended in May 2007, so by the time the tour was over, my four years would be complete. Kendra and I started to consider the possibility of getting out early, in part because when I returned to Florida for a couple of Navy band gigs, it was complete pandemonium. The crowds were bigger and rowdier. Students rushed the stage and started a mosh pit. Kids were crowd surfing. Security was called in, and at least one concert was stopped early.

"We can't send you back into high schools," the Navy said. "We don't know what to do with you."

I didn't know what to do with me either. When I was first

eliminated from *American Idol*, I had no idea what might happen next. It wasn't until I had my personal phone again that the calls starting coming in. I didn't find out until later that superstar songwriter Diane Warren, whom I met during my time on the show, was working to get me a deal with Curb Records.

Meanwhile I was asking people, "Can I really have a career outside of the Navy?"

Someone from Washington talked to me about switching from the music program to doing public relations for the Navy, maybe even attend Officer Candidate School. At the same time, I was receiving attention from record labels, so I decided to pay back the $8,000 and leave early.

Around this time—between the *American Idol* finale and the tour rehearsals—was when things went sour for me, both personally and spiritually. I was focused so much on my future music career that I ignored everything else. I don't remember anything Kendra said to me back then. She was trying to regroup the family, because Chloe and McKayla hadn't been together for the entire time I was on *Idol*. Kendra reunited the girls in Oklahoma at her parents' house. I, however, didn't see any of them for the next several weeks.

While Blake and Jordin were busy doing media, the rest of us started rehearsing for the tour. We worked on group numbers and were able to choose a solo performance from our time on the show. (I chose "Blaze of Glory.") We filled out the setlist with numbers we hadn't performed on *Idol*. For example, Gina Glocksen and I sang "It's Your Love," a duet by country artists Tim McGraw and Faith Hill.

The show moved all of the tour participants into a fancy hotel while we rehearsed. I was in a giant, luxurious room by myself. During the day we practiced; at night we hung out together, going to nightclubs and concerts.

My spiritual life was really starting to slip. The first thing to go was my Bible reading. It was gone before the tour started. The world was offered to me, and for the most part, I accepted. We were at a show one night in LA when someone ordered me a beverage with vodka. I was not a drinker at all, but they gave me this cocktail, and I immediately thought, *This is delicious!*

The truth is that my judgment was already compromised. Earlier in the evening I had unknowingly consumed a marijuana brownie. Everyone was in my hotel room before we went to the club, eating chips and talking. When they all left to get ready, I saw a brownie on a plate, and I ate it. No big deal, right? That's when I noticed that my mouth was very dry.

One of my fellow contestants called my room. "Phil, is there a brownie up there?"

There *was* a brownie. "I ate it."

I was already stoned by the time I arrived at the club.

When someone handed me that delicious cocktail, I'd never had anything like it before—or at least that's what it felt like. I just kept drinking. I didn't feel anything unusual, but when I tried to stand up, it was obvious that I was completely wasted. I don't remember much about that night, but

I can recall little fragments, such as the actress Helen Hunt being there.

From there we went to another club, and that's where I passed out. It was a place called Les Deux, and Paula Abdul's boyfriend at the time was one of the owners. There we mingled with people like Ryan Cabrera, who was a big pop star. I think some folks took pictures of me passed out, and Ryan was trying to delete the photos off people's phones. Paula's boyfriend ended up turning the lights off where I was. They were both protecting me.

Finally, they waved down a cab and Chris Richardson lifted me up on his shoulder and carried me outside. Chris is a strong guy; he's a weightlifter and former football player. At the time I probably weighed 170 pounds.

The cab driver, however, was not having it. "No, he's drunk. He's going to throw up in my taxi."

"He won't," Chris replied. "But if he does we'll pay for it."

Of course I did. I puked all over his taxi.

When we returned to the hotel, they loaded me onto a baggage cart and wheeled me up to my room. I woke up the next morning in my boxers. I have no idea how my clothes came off. I was lying on the floor, not in my bed, and I remember thinking, *I'm a worship pastor. What in the world just happened to me?* I called several of my life mentors.

"I need you guys to pray for me," I said. I shared some of the details: "I got wasted last night. I didn't see it coming. I've got to get back on track."

I didn't get drunk again, but my eyes started wandering

to different vices. The temptation to get high still lingered, because I remembered how much I enjoyed it. I didn't do any drugs from that point on . . . or did I?

My scattered memory led to the first time I ever lied to my wife. At one point during the tour, Kendra and I were at a restaurant with Chris Sligh and his wife, Sarah. Chris was talking about how funny it was to see me drunk. I think Kendra was a little bit ashamed, but she was laughing along because it seemed like a one-time thing.

Chris was laughing because he'd seen me trashed. In fact, I'm pretty sure he's the one who waved down the cab. TMZ cameras are everywhere in LA, and they carried me out the back door so TMZ wouldn't see me. Again, the people with me were trying to protect me, because it could have been controversial if someone in the media had seen me carried out.

At the restaurant with the Slighs, Kendra said, "I've never seen Phil drunk."

"If you think that's funny," Chris replied, "you should see him when he's high."

Was Chris talking about the pot brownie, or later that night at the club?

Kendra looked at me. "Phil, did you get high?"

"No," I said. It was a bald-faced lie.

My spiritual decline began with a lack of Bible reading and a nearly nonexistent prayer life. Next to go was my personal behavior. As we finished up the rehearsals, I was already acting flirty with other women. I hugged them, kissed them on the cheek. I was definitely more comfortable with them than I should have been. Barriers of intimacy were coming down. Up to that point, I'd stuck to a personal rule that I would never be alone in a room with a woman who wasn't my wife, but that rule no longer existed. Kendra wasn't around for the rehearsals. We weren't talking every day. We weren't really fighting; we just weren't connecting.

We were busy. Too busy.

———

By the time the *American Idol* tour began in July 2007, I was in full-on diva mode. The first three shows were in Florida—my world. By the third date, in Jacksonville, I was in another dimension. I acted like a star. We did interviews with all the local news outlets, and they all gave me great reviews. I was a standout in my own mind.

The production spent about a week in Florida before the first show. I wasn't drinking at this point, but let's just say that the alcohol was flowing. The tour kicked off in the city of Sunrise, near Miami, and we spent several days there polishing the show before we opened. We also spent plenty of time together on the beaches.

After the Jacksonville show, the tour headed west across the southern states and up the West Coast. From there we zigzagged through the Midwest. The night of our Chicago performance, Gina Glocksen's boyfriend surprised her by proposing onstage right after our duet.

Blake Lewis headlined the first set and Jordin, as the winner, closed out the second set. My big number occurred right after the intermission, when I rose up from beneath the stage, surrounded by several of the *Idol* girls, and delivered a soulful, Ray Charles–style version of "America the Beautiful." I wore my Navy uniform, and it was a giant, show-stopping moment. I wasn't the star of the show by any means, but I felt like one at that moment. I don't think I was conceited as much as I was drifting away from my previous life. I didn't like myself at all, and I definitely didn't like the way I was behaving.

In my head, Christian music wasn't interested in me; the church wasn't interested in me; but the country music industry *was* coming to me. I actually had a surprise encounter with country singer Tim McGraw when the *Idol* finalists went to New York City to close the NASDAQ stock exchange. The tour had the night off, so Kendra and I decided to go on a date and spend some time together.

We were headed back to our hotel when Kendra said it would be nice to take a carriage ride through Central Park, but first she needed to use the restroom. We ducked into the Ritz-Carlton, and I was waiting for Kendra in the lobby when someone called out my name. That wasn't uncommon at the time, so I turned toward the voice, assuming someone wanted an autograph or a photo.

There stood Tim McGraw, wearing a baseball cap. He shook my hand and introduced himself, even though I recognized him immediately. He seemed genuinely excited to run into me. He insisted that Kendra and I go to the dining room to meet his wife.

While Kendra talked with Faith Hill about relocating to Nashville, Tim discussed my upcoming move to country music. He kept bragging on Faith and how she was the best singer in the world. We had a great time. Before we left, Tim leaned into me and said, "Phil, the secret to great country music is honesty. If you're lying, they're going to call your bluff and you won't last. Be honest. Be you."

Problem was, I wasn't sure who Phil Stacey was anymore.

I was happily married and loved my family, but now I was in yet another strange dimension. The television audience had seen my wife and kids, they saw me meet my newborn daughter, but on the *Idol* tour nobody respected the fact that I was married. I was constantly hit on by girls. I wore my wedding ring, but nobody cared.

I wasn't too worried, at least not at first. I'd convinced myself that I was a rock—a human oak tree who could say no to temptation even when most other guys might struggle. But these thoughts were coming from a guy who'd forgotten how to pray and read the Bible. Before long I'd struck up a friendship with a girl on the tour. I was friends with everybody, but I spent quite a bit of time with this particular girl. We talked constantly.

Before long, boundaries started to blur. At first I didn't think anything of it, but I should have known better.

CHAPTER 14

DARK PHIL

———

THE TOUR PERFORMERS all traveled by bus, and after each show we'd drive overnight to the next venue. Once we arrived I tried to catch a few hours of sleep, but before long I had to get up and meet with the media, go to sound check, and grab some food. Before I knew it, it was time to perform again. Jordin Sparks and Blake Lewis were busy working on their debut albums, which meant recording in the midst of the tour. Whenever we had a day off, they both flew to LA to spend a few hours in the studio. They always made it back in time for the next show.

As the only teenage performers, Jordin and Sanjaya had to have family members accompany them on the tour. Kendra, however, wasn't even allowed on the bus. If we wanted to spend time together as a family, Kendra had to follow the tour caravan in a car, driving overnight with a three-year-old and an infant. When we finally met up, she was invariably exhausted and upset. I can only imagine what it was like to drive around the country with two young kids in the back seat. Whenever we arrived at the next venue, Kendra would say, "Phil, I need you to watch the kids. I've got to get some sleep." But I couldn't watch our daughters either, or at least that's what I told her. "I've got to sleep too," I'd say. "I've got a show tonight." It was awful. We called this season in my life Dark Phil, because it wasn't characteristic of me at all. I was in a spiritual haze.

You know how some couples settle into a comfortable routine? Well, ours was tense and definitely *uncomfortable:* Snap at Kendra; get snapped at by Kendra. Kendra leaves the road; I'm at peace. Kendra comes back on the road; I'm in chaos. Kendra leaves the road; I'm at peace again.

Part of me really wanted Kendra on that tour. She didn't want to be on the road, but I think she felt like she needed to be there. She had no idea.

Nearly two months into the tour, I began to develop a serious attraction to one of the women who frequently traveled with us on the road. (For privacy purposes, I'll call her "Jane.") I'd convinced myself that everything was cool. "You don't understand," I'd tell people. "I'm an oak. I say no to people every day. You've got nothing to worry about." And I managed to keep it that way for a while, but I started to entertain certain inappropriate thoughts in my head, especially when I met flirty fans on the road.

Kendra showed up at one of the venues and was looking for me. "Have you seen Phil?" she asked one of the other performers, who responded, "He's off with his girlfriend somewhere." All the other singers were friends with Kendra at this point, so I think the comment was made as a joke.

No one got upset; they all thought it was funny. Kendra was laughing about it too. I learned about the incident later, and at the time they were right. Jane and I *weren't* being inappropriate. We *were* just buddies. But the laughter made me wonder, *Why does Kendra think that's so funny?*

Kendra eventually found me in the catering room, and I wasn't with Jane. "I was told you were with your girlfriend," she said with a giggle. Meanwhile, I was thinking, *Why is that so impossible to believe?* I don't know what that incident did to unleash my messed-up reasoning, but I began to wonder, *What if she was my girlfriend?*

I allowed myself to think of Jane as more than just a buddy, to consider the possibility of something more. I noticed her looks. The way she smiled at me. *Why couldn't she be my girlfriend? Is it because she's too pretty to be my girlfriend?*

A wise man doesn't entertain thoughts like that, and he definitely doesn't dwell on them. Because when you ponder certain thoughts too much and for too long, there's a chance that the thing you thought would never happen might happen after all.

My next move was to try to justify the thoughts in my head. *King David's eyes wandered, so maybe God understands.* My thought process was completely irrational and, frankly, pretty dumb, but something happened to shift the relationship from being solely in my head to being *real.* I started viewing Jane in a new way, and she started looking at me differently. She picked up on what I was sending.

My wife noticed it first. Kendra made a comment about how Jane looked at me during an *Idol* event, and I wanted to see for myself what Kendra was talking about. Big mistake. When I started watching Jane to see how she was looking at me, she noticed that I was looking back at her. Our eyes met. She was into me, and I was into her. It was awkward, and still neither of us would admit what was happening.

The tension finally came to a head when Jane asked, "Are we going to talk about this?"

"About what?" I replied.

I absolutely knew what she was saying, but I didn't want to acknowledge it. If I pretended that our feelings didn't exist, maybe I could keep everything in the land of make-believe. My plan was naive, of course. Before long, I was sending Jane flirty text messages. She knew exactly what I was feeling. We each knew what the other wanted. It was all a game until it wasn't.

By the last month of the tour, most everyone around us figured that something inappropriate was happening. We were definitely too comfortable around each other.

Let me be clear: My actions were unacceptable, my thoughts inexcusable. Jesus said in Matthew 5:28 that if you even look at a woman lustfully, you've committed adultery in your heart. Well, I did exactly that. Guilty as charged. I was dancing with danger, and it could have destroyed me. As terrible as it is to say, it was an enticing, romantic evil. I wanted it.

The impending end of the tour probably clouded my thinking even more. *If I'm going to do this, now is the time.* Fortunately, the time I was most tempted to pursue physical involvement with Jane, God gave me the strength to walk away. I'm still not sure what prevented us from entering a full-blown affair, but I'm thankful we didn't.

Unfortunately, that wasn't the end of it. I was still torn about the relationship. Jane had become my girlfriend in almost every way, and it's only by God's grace that I finally came to my senses.

Wherever we performed, I knew people in the audience saw me as wholesome. Some of them knew I was a worship pastor; I'd received letters about it. Couples watched me sing on *American Idol,* and they saw my marriage and family as something to emulate. "Thank you for your ministry," they told me.

When I read those fan letters, I felt like such a hypocrite. I wasn't much of a Christian anymore. Even if I was, I was a pretty bad example. My only comfort is knowing that I didn't have a physical affair. My mind and my heart went there, and this Dark Phil period affected me spiritually for a long time. (I'm convinced that all the people who were praying for me helped hold me up in the end, and I'm grateful for every one of them.)

At times I wondered if my behavior and mindset even mattered. There were times when I didn't feel remotely bad about my thoughts and behavior, mostly because I was living in my "alternate dimension"—a reality where nothing could affect me. *Who cares if I lose some church gigs? Whatever. I'm making more money each week than I made all of last year. Who cares about a little bad publicity if I get a divorce? If I get a divorce right now, if my wife leaves me, all it means is that I'll be starting country music with a fresh slate.*

That's right—the possibility of divorce was floating around in my head. We never discussed it out loud, but Kendra started making offhand comments about our relationship. "I really don't feel this right now," she said, and I just knew what she was talking about. And she still didn't know the full extent of what had happened.

———

Sometime during the *American Idol* tour, Chaz Corzine introduced me to the folks from Lyric Street Records. The company's president was there, and they wanted me to record a demo after I finished the tour. This meant we'd be relocating from Jacksonville to Nashville.

As soon as I returned to Jacksonville, I returned my Navy signing bonus, filled out all my paperwork, and went into the reserves. In a matter of weeks, I'd moved my family to Franklin, a suburb just south of Nashville. Everything was happening according to schedule.

Probably the biggest surprise I received was a huge bill from my lawyers in New York. I had no idea why I owed this money, so I called one of my attorneys and asked, "What is this bill for? I haven't even spoken to you guys."

"We negotiated a recording contract for you."

I found out that Diane Warren, one of the most successful songwriters in pop music, was working to get me a record deal so that I could record some of her songs. Now, I absolutely love Diane Warren's songwriting, so I would have been down with it, but nobody had even mentioned the negotiations to me. This massive bill was the first I'd heard of it.

I met Diane through *American Idol*, and I sang one of her compositions, "I Could Not Ask for More," on the show. Diane told me she loved the performance and my voice, and I spent some time with her. She took me into her studio, where I recorded demos for some of her new songs. One time when I was at her studio, she said, "Phil, I've got to go. I'm meeting up with Paul McCartney."

The person I was hanging with had a meeting with Paul McCartney—how cool is that? Of course, that's Diane Warren's everyday life. I still have copies of those demos, including "Borrowed Angels," which Kristin Chenoweth also recorded.

At one point Diane told me, "I'm going to get you a record deal," but I didn't think she was serious. After all, I was just one singer in a room full of them. I never heard another word about it until I received that bill. Apparently Diane had contacted the record label and told them they needed to sign me. I never met or spoke with anybody from the label, but I discovered that Diane Warren's recommendation alone was enough to seal the deal.

When I told my attorney that I had no knowledge of any negotiations, he understood completely. "That's true," he said. "We just never talked about it. Don't worry about that bill."

Jay DeMarcus from the group Rascal Flatts had also helped me make contacts with yet another record label. Jay and I were connected through our alma mater and some mutual friends, but I was working with Chaz now. Chaz negotiated a contract for me with Lyric Street Records, so that's who I went with.

───

The *Idol* tour ended in September, and I was in a haze. I still had feelings for Jane, and we continued to share inappropriate messages fairly regularly.

Kendra didn't know the full story yet, but she could tell that *something* was going on. "You've got to let her go," she pleaded. "Delete her number. Erase her photos. I need you to do that for me."

"That's ridiculous," I replied. "What are you talking about?"

I was still in denial. I wasn't ready to let go. Nothing physical had happened with Jane, so I told my wife that she had nothing to worry about.

"Get rid of her," Kendra insisted.

So I kind of did, but I kind of didn't. I deleted Jane's number and her photos, but I kept her email. I still had feelings for this girl. Something had to give, and soon.

A few days later, it did.

I was back home, but I didn't want to see my wife or kids because they reminded me too much of the real world. That's when I realized that I'd fallen in love with my fake world. *Huh? What was I thinking?* In that instant, it struck me just how much better my real life was compared to the fake on-the-road world. That's the best way I can describe what happened in my mind. The wool over my eyes fell away. The haze finally disappeared, and I could see clearly again.

In 1 Timothy 4:2, the Bible talks about hypocrites whose consciences have been seared as with a hot iron. I felt that my conscience had cooked to the point where I'd become oblivious to my downward spiritual spiral.

Romans 1:28 describes how God gave people over to a depraved mind, and that's where I'd been. In my heart, Jane and I *did* have an affair. In my head, we *were* intimate.

It was one of my girls' birthdays that day, and I suddenly viewed the true condition of my soul. *What am I doing? How did I get so lost? What just happened?* I felt as if a supernatural struggle was happening inside me.

I fell on the floor in my living room and began to repent. *God, I'm sorry. God, I'm sorry.* I recognized that God had given me the *American Idol* opportunity, and the first things I'd done were sign a country music record deal and chase after a girl who wasn't my wife. Why? That wasn't me. Even when I was smoking weed in high school, I still loved Jesus and spent time with Him every day. Now I had disregarded the Lord for the last few months—completely disregarded Him—even as He'd given me the gift of this platform.

I've spoiled this opportunity, I thought. *There's nothing I can do that will be successful. God can't bless this experience anymore because I've squandered it.*

Around that same time, I received a long message from a gospel singer named Michael English. I had never met the man, but I was a big fan of his and knew that he'd experienced his own personal struggles in the 1990s. "Hey Phil," he wrote, "I see God's hand on your life, and I wanted to send you a letter to warn you about some of the traps the devil's going to lay for you. . . ."

"I see exactly what you're talking about," I replied. "Thank you so much." While we've never connected in person, we've written each other several times. I can't tell you how timely that first message was. It arrived right when I was coming out of my fog. And if I thought the *American Idol* tour was rough, I *really* wasn't prepared for touring in the world of country music.

I sent one more email to Jane, to officially end any further contact. I told her, "I don't know what happened to me, but I just woke up. It's like I've been asleep, like I've been dreaming. It started as a joke; it turned into something real; and now it's a nightmare. And right now, in this moment, I can't believe the way I treated you. I'm so sorry. Please forgive me."

I never heard back, and she never contacted me again.

CHAPTER 15

COUNTRY MUSIC

I HAD RECOGNIZED MY SIN, but I wasn't quite ready to confront it. I had an attitude of repentance, but how far did that go? Did I need to tell Kendra about everything with Jane? Even though nothing happened from a physical standpoint, my heart and mind had been unfaithful.

Our relationship was not in a good place, but suddenly I wanted us to make it work more than ever. I didn't want to lose my marriage, but if I told Kendra everything, I feared that's exactly what would happen.

Moreover, I wasn't convinced that I needed to confess *everything*. I was looking for advice, looking for answers, but I was reading from sources that *I* wanted to read. If there was an author or an excuse out there that gave me permission to avoid a confrontation—to avoid facing my behavior—then I was going to take it.

In the meantime, I needed to record my debut album right away. Lyric Street Records brought in outside song-writers. They chose the songs. I cut the album in Nashville, working with a Grammy-winning songwriter and producer extraordinaire named Wayne Kirkpatrick. I spent quite a bit of time with Wayne. He's the sweetest guy you'll ever meet, but he's also very intimidating in the studio. He expects you to deliver right away, so if you're not good, you're going to have a tough time with Wayne. He doesn't like to use Auto-Tune to fix a singer's pitch problems, and he doesn't like to record digitally. He prefers analog, which means recording directly to an old-school, two-inch-tape machine.

Recording digitally allows the performer to take virtually unlimited passes at a song. That's not the case with analog tape. I remember on one track, Wayne gave me three takes, and at the end of those three takes he said, "All right, I think we're good."

I had just finished singing the song three times—each time all the way through. Most other producers would say, "All right, we're warmed up; let's hit the first verse."

Not Wayne. "We're good," he said.

"Are we going to start recording now?" I asked.

"I already got three takes," Wayne replied.

This was not going the way I had hoped. "Bro, I'd like to sing it more than three times."

"If you can't sing it in three takes, you can't sing it."

I think he was joking.

The album was simply titled *Phil Stacey*. To be honest, I didn't like the finished product. All I could hear was the strain in my voice. At the same time I was recording the album, I was busy doing radio station tours. We completed the first three songs right away since Lyric Street had already chosen the lead single. Because it often takes a while for a song to climb the charts, they sent the single out to radio stations in advance while I finished up the album.

That meant I was on the road for four or five days at a time promoting the record at different country stations around the country. The same day I came home, I went back into the studio to record a couple more songs. By that point my voice just felt dead.

When I heard the completed recording, I wrote a bunch of notes regarding some things I wanted to change and sent them to Wayne and Doug Howard, the vice president of A&R at Lyric Street. To Wayne's credit, he called me back right away.

"Hey, Phil," he said, "you just heard the final master. It's done."

It was too late to make any changes. I was devastated, but they wanted to put out the record as soon as possible. They wanted to capitalize on the wave of promotion I'd received from *American Idol*.

I avoided the final product for years after that, but Wayne, he loved it. And Doug Howard, who looks like a young Colonel Sanders and is one of the kindest men I've ever met, insisted, "Phil, it's a great record." I had no choice but to trust his professional assessment. Lyric Street Records was a subsidiary of the Disney Music Group and home to artists like Rascal Flatts, SHeDAISY, and Billy Ray Cyrus. The company was trying to defend the recording, but I couldn't bring myself to listen to it. I didn't like my single; I didn't like the song. But they had chosen it, so I had to sing that song, and I had to find meaning in it.

I'm the kind of performer who has trouble singing a song unless I find meaning in it, and the message of "If You Didn't Love Me" was pretty straightforward: "If you didn't love me, then I don't know how I could do this." The lyrics were perfectly appropriate for my life right then. If Kendra didn't love me, I would fall apart. At this point I was leaning on her support more than I ever had before.

After years of avoiding that album, I finally listened to it again all the way through a couple of years ago. And you know what? Doug Howard was right—it *is* a good album! All those years later I thought, *This isn't bad.*

The *Phil Stacey* album introduced me to the world of country music, and that world was definitely not what I imagined. In country music, almost anything goes. For example, I recall performing at a big music festival with a country artist who had a bunch of massive hits. A couple of my band members and I were on his tour bus after the show when some girls stepped onto the bus. They were beautiful girls, scantily dressed and very flirtatious. Despite my protests, one of them walked over and sat on my lap.

She promptly called her mother and said, "You won't believe whose lap I'm sitting on right now. It's Phil Stacey!"

"Can I talk to him?" her mother asked.

She handed me the phone, and this girl's mother began crying almost immediately. "My daughter is only sixteen," she said. "Will you please make sure she's safe? I know you're a pastor."

This girl looked at least twenty-one, and I can guarantee that none of the other guys on the bus knew she was sixteen. I don't know about all the experiences other country artists have with girls, but we had girls from *Playboy* show up at our concerts. This was the world we lived in. Everybody was drinking, and it was a highly sexualized environment.

Kendra and I were attending an awards show when a well-known industry executive brought us a couple shots of whisky.

"No thanks," we said. "We don't drink."

This guy looked at us like we were from another planet. "Well, then you can't be in country music."

I was taken aback. "What?"

"If you don't drink whisky, then you can't be in country music," he repeated.

I know he was joking. Mostly. I also know there was a bit of truth in what he was saying. This man had a lot of power and influence over my career—over *a lot* of country music careers. He opened a lot of doors for me, and for that I am very grateful. He eventually chuckled and walked away with the drinks, and he still kept giving me gigs. In other words, he wasn't really serious that evening, but I will admit that if the same thing happened at a different time in my life, I probably would have taken that drink.

That incident wasn't the only time I felt uncomfortable. In one city, a radio station program director told me, "I'm not going to play your single unless you take me to a strip club." *Well, I guess I'm not going to get my single played here.* I'd just spent months on *American Idol*, and no one involved with the show ever pressured me to go to a strip club. There was never a time when a girl stepped onto our tour bus and sat on my lap. Turns out that *American Idol* was more wholesome than the world of country music, at least from my perspective.

You could openly talk about God and the Bible in the country music world and nobody flinched. You could also be halfway through your bottle of Jack Daniel's and say, "Man, I just love Jesus so much."

My first single was doing well—or at least that's what I thought. "If You Didn't Love Me" went to number twenty-eight on Billboard's Country Songs chart, and *Phil Stacey* hit number eight on the Country Albums chart, but the sales were apparently a disappointment to my record label. Keep in mind that the album came out in 2008, in the middle of a national financial crisis, so it wasn't like a whole bunch of records were selling.

Lyric Street Records talked about releasing a second single. I didn't like any of the proposed songs, so we ended up re-recording a new, radio-friendly version of "No Way Around a River," produced by Jay DeMarcus. Lyric Street also heard about a patriotic song called "Old Glory" that I'd written while I was in the Navy. We never recorded it for my album, but the song was a big hit at my concerts. "Maybe we should send that out as a single," the label executives said.

"Old Glory" was eventually released on iTunes, but we never could settle on a second single for radio. Before long, the album sales had fallen off. Without another single, there was no more momentum, and without momentum . . . well, you get the picture.

I talked to Doug Howard at Lyric Street about how I didn't feel comfortable in the country music genre. Spending a year in that world convinced me that I'd rather switch over to Christian music. One defining moment occurred when I participated in a panel discussion at the Gospel Music Association's 2008 event in Nashville. Joining me on the panel were singers Rebecca St. James and Mark Hall from the group Casting Crowns. I don't recall what the session was called, but I remember the audience asking me questions about *American Idol* and my experiences in country music.

After the session was over, Mark Hall and I sat alone at a table in the hotel conference room. I don't know if Mark remembers our discussion that day, but it had a tremendous impact on my career. Mark is also a pastor, and I'd made it clear that I was struggling.

"Phil, why are you doing country music?" he asked.

"Well," I said, "those were the opportunities that came to me, so I figured that's where God wanted me."

By this point I'd emerged from my time in the spiritual wilderness. The "hate mail" had stopped. My prayer life was back. I was attending church regularly. I'd repented before God for my behavior (though Kendra still didn't know). Now I was thinking, *God gave me this opportunity; I need to use it for His glory.*

"You're hoping that God could use the platform of country music to reach people for Christ," Mark said. It was a statement, but it felt like a question.

"For sure!"

That's why I was in country music—I performed alongside artists like Lady A, Sugarland, and Trace Adkins, and I'd had several chances to talk to people about Christ and pray with some leading country artists in the midst of their personal struggles. When I wasn't touring with these bigger groups, I played my own shows in bars and clubs. I thought I'd been given a great opportunity for ministry.

"Okay, that's great," Mark said. "So you're doing stuff for Jesus?"

"Yeah, I'm getting to pray for people behind the scenes."

Mark leaned in. "How is that working out?"

"I don't know," I replied. "What do you mean?"

"Well, do you ever do altar calls?"

"Altar calls in a *bar*? At a country music concert?" I was puzzled. "I don't do those."

"What about your testimonial time during your concert where you talk about Jesus?"

"I'm not really doing that either," I said. "But I do sing 'Hold Me Jesus' by Rich Mullins at every concert."

"So let me get this straight," Mark said. "You're hanging your ministry on the idea that someone will hear that one song you sing or read one interview where you mention your faith, and it will inspire them to seek the gospel and surrender their lives to Christ?"

Mark was as real as it gets. He wasn't attacking me; he was asking a very sincere question.

"I guess that's what I'm hoping for," I agreed. "I'm hoping for my concerts to somehow influence people to become a Christian."

Mark viewed church performances as an opportunity to equip the body of Christ. "When we do a concert," he said, "the majority of people who attend are believers, but those same believers are connected to people who are lost. What if we could, with our music, inspire an army of believers to preach the gospel? What if we could inspire them to bring people into the church, where they could learn how to become disciples of Christ?"

My heart resonated with Mark's words. While I know there is a place for believers in mainstream music, and I do know several who have used their platform wisely, I also knew that I was called to be a *minister*, not just a singer. I realized that if I could help ten believers reach ten more, I could have more Kingdom impact than if I had a thriving career as a country artist. His logic made sense to me.

Mark asked a final question: "Phil, if you did a concert for 40,000 people with your one Christian song and nothing ever came from it, or you sang at a church in front of twenty people and convinced those twenty to be salt and light in their communities—at which performance did you do the more effective work for the gospel?"

"In my opinion," I answered, "I guess I would have to say the church performance."

"I'm glad you're doing what you're doing," Mark said. "I just wanted to challenge you as a Christian brother, and I want to encourage you because I believe God has chosen you for something. You just need to know why you're doing it."

His words struck me. He was right; I could've been more effective for the Kingdom. Whenever I did interviews, reporters asked me about my *American Idol* experience and what it was like. They didn't ask me about Jesus, they didn't talk about my church background. Why should they? My only demonstration of faith was to include a Jesus song in my setlist. Anybody can do that.

Mark had definitely given me something to think about. I left that Gospel Music Association event and had a conversation with Chaz, my manager.

"I think I'd like to do a Christian record," I told him.

I expressed the same desire to Lyric Street Records. "That's not something we do," Doug Howard said. "That's not something we can do together."

Randy Goodman, the company president, told me, "Phil, I really admire what you're doing in holding to your faith; I admire that you didn't want any songs on your album that compromised your beliefs. But it's challenging in country music to give you liftoff with nothing to talk about."

In other words, while uplifting lyrics are fine, the record company also wanted songs that made listeners pay attention—perhaps a jarring topic, something with a little controversy. Give the audience something to talk about. My album definitely didn't have that.

I was on the road a week or two later when Chaz called to tell me that Lyric Street had decided to dissolve my contract. They weren't going to release a second single, and they weren't going to pick up their option for a second album. My first record deal was done. Would it be my only one?

Chaz was bummed because he thought I was losing my best chance for artistic success. He didn't know that I'd been praying about this exact situation. *God, if You don't want me in country music, please open the door for me to leave.*

CHAPTER 16

FORGIVEN

————

MY COUNTRY ALBUM had sold enough copies to break even, but I didn't make a profit from that record. I didn't know what would happen next, but I still had some money in the bank, so I felt confident that I had time to figure it out.

In the meantime, I still had concert dates to fulfill. Some of the dates were scheduled long before my record came out. (Being a finalist on *American Idol* typically gets you at least a year's worth of gigs right off the bat.) As the months passed, I started canceling my country dates and began booking churches instead. I thought I'd be able to bring my band with me, but churches don't pay the same, so the full band dates started slowing down in the fall of 2008.

I spoke to Chaz about doing Christian music because he's been involved in it for years. He jumped right in, talking about potential opportunities, making plans, maybe setting up some songwriting sessions. He wanted to make things happen, but I was hesitant. *Do I even want to be in commercial music?*

As I've said before, I didn't really want to be famous. I'd experienced that, and it was miserable. During my season on *Idol* and the months that followed, when so many people recognized me, I couldn't walk through an airport without being accosted or hugged by random strangers. They wanted to take photos with me, and I wanted to be polite. You try to stay positive with everyone, because you know that the moment you say, "Why are you hugging me?" it's going to be on the internet. Everybody will think you're a jerk. So I tried to be polite, but it was draining.

My wife and I even had stalkers. They found out where we lived. One guy convinced Kendra that he was a station program director and she gave him my cell phone number. I was on the road somewhere, and he called to tell me that he was standing outside of my house and he knew that I was gone.

"Do you want me to go in and watch your family and make sure they're okay?" he asked.

"Get away from my house," I replied.

There are plenty of great fans. There are also some strange ones. It had little to do with me and more to do with them latching on to *somebody*. (Paula Abdul had it far worse—an obsessed fan committed suicide outside her home.) It creeped me out because my family was there in the house. During the annual Country Music Association festival, people stood in the street waiting for me to come out of my house so they could take photos.

It took about a year for that to wear off, for the next crop of *American Idol* finalists to take over. I haven't heard from the strange fans in years. I did hear from a different one about two years ago, when he came out of the woodwork on Facebook: "Hey, just wanted to say 'hi' to you. Miss you so much."

The demands from fans and the months of touring bred negativity inside of me, but the only person who ever noticed it was Kendra. She saw the sadness in me. "Whatever you want to do," she said, "I'll support you. I'm behind you."

I desperately needed to know that Kendra believed in me, because there was something we still needed to talk about.

In October 2008, I was invited to be a part of a tribute performance for Christian music legend Michael W. Smith. Sitting in the audience was Terry Hemmings, the president of Reunion Records—Michael W. Smith's record label. Afterward Chaz texted me, saying that Terry wanted to meet with me. Terry asked me, "Why didn't you want to do country music? Is moving to Christian music a weird shift for you?"

He wanted to hear my story for himself. We eventually scheduled writing sessions, and Reunion signed me to my second record deal. At this point my whole life was changing and rearranging, and I was focused more on ministry than record sales.

It had been about a year since I'd last done any ministry work, and I decided that if I was going to enter that world again, I needed to be completely transparent in my personal and spiritual life. I needed to have a conversation with Kendra.

I was still on active reserve with the U.S. Navy and performed occasional events for them. In November 2008, the Navy flew me to Naples, Italy, to sing for a bunch of dignitaries. Our tenth wedding anniversary was coming up, so I decided to bring Kendra along and make the trip a special celebration.

We spent about a week in Naples, where I rehearsed and performed, and then just the two of us went on to Rome. I remembered how much I treasured this woman, but I also knew that I had kept something from her for more than a year. We were staying at a beautiful hotel in Rome, and it was late, sometime after midnight. Kendra was already down for the night, but I couldn't sleep. I loved my wife dearly, yet there was no emotional intimacy between us. Our connection was gone, and I was the one who'd destroyed it.

It was eating me up inside. I had to tell her.

I don't know how long I lay in bed, staring at the ceiling. Finally I turned on the light. "Kendra," I said, "can I talk to you?"

"Sure, what is it?"

"I need to tell you about this girl."

Kendra would typically lie there while I talked, but this time she sat up immediately. She knew right away that this was serious.

I'd debated having this conversation. If I was the only one feeling the emptiness and lack of intimacy, then I was about to dump a huge burden on her. I dreaded how she might respond.

By now I knew that Kendra was with me, but I didn't know if she would want to stay with me once I finished talking. I'd been hiding something from her for a long time, and the last time we'd spoken about it, I had insisted, "You've got nothing to worry about."

It was a lie of course.

"I'm about to go into this new season of ministry," I said, "and I don't know if I can. I don't know if I'm *allowed*. I've forgiven myself partially, but you're a part of me, and you don't even know the whole story. I have to tell you the whole story."

I said the woman's name, and I'm sure Kendra was ready for me to tell her that I'd had an affair. I could see the fear on her face. I confessed everything, and I mean *everything*. I told her about the inappropriate messages, and that I'd deleted them all. I described the emotional connection I'd developed with Jane, how I'd allowed myself to desire her and thus betrayed my marriage. I'd betrayed Kendra. I'd sinned against God and against my wife.

I said I'd kept this information from her because I'd convinced myself that it didn't affect *us*. We both knew better. I apologized for what I'd done, for not telling her the truth, and for not telling her sooner. I don't know how long I went on, but it seemed like I talked for an hour while Kendra sat there listening.

There are many ways she could have reacted, but Kendra's response was short and sweet. "I forgive you," she said. She kissed me on the cheek, rolled over, and went back to sleep. It was grace personified, and it was a wake-up call. It felt like what happens when you bring your sins to Christ. He says, "I forgive you," and then they're gone. Kendra never brought it up again.

The burden that hung heavy over my heart for more than a year was immediately lifted. That night it felt as if God spoke to me about my future. What I heard was basically the story of Samson—how Samson betrayed God, betrayed Israel, betrayed his people, and did many stupid things. Samson deserved to die, yet in his last moments he repented and asked God to restore his strength. God is merciful by nature, and He answered Samson's final prayer.

God wants to see us fulfill our destiny. Here I was, thinking it was too late for me to experience what Christ had in store for me after *American Idol.* I'd basically thrown away an entire year, yet that night God reminded me that He was capable of restoring the time I'd lost.

Dr. Mauldin had attended one of the dates on the *American Idol* tour. When I took him backstage after the show, he asked me, "Phil, are you okay?"

"I don't know, Doc," I replied. "What do you mean?"

"I just want you to know that I've had a heavy burden for you and I'm praying for you," he said. "And it's not just about *American Idol*. I feel like there's a spiritual stronghold against you, and I'm praying for you."

I told Dr. Mauldin how much I appreciated his concern, but I didn't tell him the real story. I didn't tell him about Jane, about the stress in my marriage, and about my plans for a career in country music. I saw him again a couple of years later, after his wife passed away, and I revealed what I had really been going through when we'd spoken during the *Idol* tour.

"I knew there was something happening," he said.

I thanked him again for his prayers, because at the time I had desperately needed them.

Once I'd been forgiven, I finally felt free to do something for Jesus again. I had signed my deal with Reunion Records and started working on my second album, *Into the Light*.

I still didn't trust myself as a songwriter, but this time I was able to contribute to the writing on several tracks. The album concluded with a stripped-down, piano-and-vocals-only version of my song "Old Glory."

Brown Bannister produced the record, and I had a great time working with him. Brown is a pastor at heart, so we would pray before each recording session, which we didn't do with my country album. I remember cutting one particular vocal with Brown, and he said, "Phil, I feel like you're singing to me."

"That's great, right, because it's personal?" I replied.

"Not really," Brown said, "because this is a lyric to Jesus, and it's a painful lyric to Jesus. What I want you to do is look into the microphone and use your imagination to picture Jesus' face, and I want you to sing to Him."

I don't know that Brown's idea resulted in a great vocal, but I will say that I love that record. I listen to it all the time.

The first single from *Into the Light* was a song I helped write called "You're Not Shaken." The label initially chose a different single, but Brown was the one who fought for "You're Not Shaken."

"All right," Reunion said. "Let's do it."

After we released that first single, I wanted to work with churches, to do something beyond being part of the Christian music industry. More importantly, I wanted to work with overseas missions.

In 2009, I was invited to participate in an outreach event in the Philippines. A missionary named Scott Rains contacted me through Facebook. "The Philippines has a big *American Idol* following," he said. "Could you help us launch an event called AsiaFest where we want to share the gospel?"

AsiaFest took place in Manila, and it was beautiful to see how these kids responded to me and how God used my notoriety from *American Idol* to bring more people to the event. Many students gave their lives to Christ at AsiaFest.

Planetshakers, a band from Australia whose songs are performed in churches all over America, led the worship, and then I performed with just my acoustic guitar. I actually sang in Tagalog, a language used in the Philippines.

It was on that stage in Manila, looking out at all these kids, that I realized just how much I loved them. I was on the other side of the world, singing for a bunch of strangers, yet my heart was filled with love for these people. I didn't know why; I concluded that it must have been a Holy Spirit thing. I wanted the best for these people. I should actually say that I wanted the best for these *individuals*, because I didn't see them as a group; I saw them as separate human beings. I felt I had a glimpse of how God sees us—individually. He singles people out. For example, in Acts 9, God tells Ananias specifically to go pray for Saul. I love that. I love that God sees every single person.

That moment onstage in Manila wasn't the first time I'd felt that Holy Spirit–inspired love for all. I'd felt it before, but it was that moment when I first *acknowledged* it. There were many years in my life when I didn't feel close to anyone. I was a loner when we moved to Wichita and I had to repeat the eighth grade. I was a loner again for most of my freshman year in college—and when I finally did make some new friends, I had to give them up. Finally, God brought me Kendra.

Along the way, I learned to be satisfied being alone. Some people are miserable sitting in a hotel room with no one else around, but I love it. It's fantastic. Sometimes I think I could go through life without acknowledging other people at all. But when I'm onstage, ministering and singing, leading worship, I experience an overwhelming sense of love for individuals in the audience. I'm making eye contact with people, and I have a deep sense of empathy for them, as if I sense what they're going through. *I will leave here tonight, but they still have to go home to whatever their situation might be.*

For a long time I was disconnected from the lives of others. I found it easy to forget about them the moment they left the room. But there's something about God's Holy Spirit that compels me to think about and pray for individuals. Ever since that moment onstage, I have sensed God's love for people, for every person in the audience. I'm just a regular guy who struggles with my issues like everyone else, but the Holy Spirit helped me grasp that there's a God who loves people more than I ever could.

About a year after my season on *American Idol*, Disney World announced the creation of a new park attraction called The American Idol Experience. For the attraction's grand opening, Disney brought in finalists from every season of the show. They booked a beautiful hotel for the past contestants and gave us VIP passes to the park.

It was a magical event—better than any time I've ever been there with my kids. We watched season seven winner David Cook sing a duet with Carrie Underwood, and they were fantastic. I was introduced to several other *American Idol* finalists, many of whom I'd seen on television but never actually met. *Idol* finalists are like members of an exclusive club, with the shared experience of returning to the "real world" afterward. It seemed like everyone at Disney World recognized us from the show.

It's actually jarring to recall just how popular *Idol* was at the time. The show was a global phenomenon. I remember returning to Florida the next year for a radio event, and I was sitting in a restaurant with a group of well-known Christian artists, including Michael W. Smith, Mac Powell from Third Day, solo artist Brandon Heath, and Mark Hall of Casting Crowns. Many of the eight artists at our table had spent the past thirty years molding and shaping Christian music. That's how influential they'd been.

When the waitress walked up to our table, she started freaking out: "You're Phil Stacey from *American Idol!*"

Michael W. Smith could only smile. "Yes, he is," he said.

They got a kick out of it, because all of these musicians had sold more records than I'll sell in my entire life. Yet I was the one our waitress recognized.

CHAPTER 17

MINISTRY AND MISSIONS

―――――――

I SPENT MONTHS ON THE ROAD singing country music, yet I never felt fulfilled by what I was doing. When I was out on the mission field, however, I felt highly fulfilled. I loved overseas ministry, and whenever I came back to America, I was convinced that I needed to do more church work and not just be part of the commercial music industry.

Still, I had plenty of wonderful opportunities thanks to Christian music. I toured first with singer Natalie Grant, then with Michael W. Smith on his New Hallelujah Tour. I joined up again with Natalie Grant and Britt Nicole on Natalie's Love Revolution Tour.

Throughout the Love Revolution Tour, I befriended all

the hosts and concert promoters. "I'm coming back to this area in a few months," I said. "I think this event is a good bridge toward getting an audience back out if you'd like to do a show together. And instead of asking for an honorarium, we can do a ticket split, so you know that you're going to make money."

I ended up doing some of the same venues on my own tour, which we called the Love Revolution 2.0 Tour. I wanted to have my own band, but I wasn't sure the endeavor would be profitable, so I decided to approach my old college—Lee University.

"I know you have a group, Second Edition, that tours during the summer," I said. "What would you think about them coming out on the road with me? We'll play some of the biggest Christian music festivals, and I'll take them into a lot of good venues. All I need you to do is provide the band and the bus. We'll even talk about Lee onstage and set up a table for the university at each venue. It can be a recruiting tool."

They agreed to it. They provided us with a bus and a band, and we toured for two months. The members of Second Edition received scholarship money and a stipend to tour during the summer; I just put them up in hotels and paid for their meals. The tour ended up doing amazingly well. It gave me the confidence I needed to move out of the traditional Christian music industry and do my own thing. There was just one problem: Because I had scheduled so many of my own shows, my booking agency dropped me.

"You arranged these dates yourself," they said, "so you really don't need us anymore. You're doing well enough on your own."

Chaz was concerned. "Phil, you can't just go doing stuff like this," he said. But at the same time, the agency wasn't finding me any new gigs. If I hadn't done it myself, I would have been sitting at home for most of that summer. Other than a couple of festival dates, I arranged all of my own shows. It got to the point where I separated completely from the music industry.

It didn't matter whether it was country music, Christian music, whatever—I wanted to leave the commercial industry behind to concentrate on ministry. God in His mercy had shown me His grace and personified it through my wife in a wonderful moment of forgiveness, so now all I wanted to do was ministry. Ticketed concerts are fine; they're just not my thing. People shouldn't have to pay in order to hear me lift up the name of Jesus. I was ready for a change.

Reunion Records was talking about the next single, about recording another album. We didn't make a ton of money on *Into the Light*, so the record company was considering an acoustic follow-up or something like that. But I was ready to move on.

"I think I'm done, guys," I said, and that was it.

I parted ways with Chaz, too. That was tough, but he's still a friend and I love him dearly. Chaz opened up many doors for me and my family, but he could tell that my priorities were changing. "It doesn't really make any sense for you to keep me," he agreed.

I had money in the bank, so I felt comfortable. I had my earnings from *Idol*, from country music, from touring. In my mind, I was rich. By the end of 2010, I was completely on my own. I had separated from the music industry to focus on ministry projects, and that's when I discovered that all of the money in my bank account had disappeared.

My first call was to my business manager. "We've been robbed," I told her.

"No, you just paid your commissions," she said.

Because I'd ended my business relationships with all my industry partners—management and booking agencies, lawyers, transportation—she had paid all the commissions and taxes I owed and closed out the accounts. There was $17 left in my bank account.

I had no concept of what I owed. All I know is that it was a lot of money, and it was all gone. Even though I have the receipts, I still don't know exactly how it happened. I owed legal fees. I owed for every contract my lawyers negotiated. I could no longer afford the business manager who'd just paid all my bills. I remember stressing out. *What in the world am I going to do?* But the very next moment it struck me: *God has got this. God is going to take care of me. He's the one who provided me with groceries when I was starving.*

The first thing I needed to do was pray, and that's when offers started coming in through my Facebook page—churches inviting me to sing. I also heard from a pastor near Kansas City who needed a temporary music minister. I'd performed at his church earlier that year on the Love Revolution 2.0 Tour, but they were going through some upheaval and he wasn't ready to bring someone in on a permanent basis.

"Phil," he said, "I'm in a really weird situation where I don't want to hire a permanent pastor because I don't know how long this position is going to be available, but I need somebody who can lead worship for me."

I wanted to help him out, so I kept my house in Nashville but moved my family to an apartment in Kansas City. We stayed there for about a year. I served as choir director, I hired my own band members, and every one of them moved to Kansas City. We'd play on a Saturday night in Wyoming and then drive overnight in order to be at church on Sunday morning.

While I was in Kansas City, another opportunity came along. Market America asked me to help them launch an entertainment company. They paid me to advise them on creating alternative methods for artists to get their music out. They wanted to figure out how to rebuild the commercial music industry, because the traditional model for selling records was in chaos.

My yearlong contract with Market America paid our bills, and my work at the church came with a salary. I only had to be there on Sundays, so I was still able to tour. It was everything I'd asked for: I had separated from the industry and was engaging in ministry all over the country—actually all over the planet, because I also traveled to other countries. I occasionally missed a Sunday, but that was okay as long as I had someone to fill in.

God had completely taken care of my family financially.

———

We spent a year in Kansas City and then moved back home to Nashville. I also returned to missions work in earnest. Along with my AsiaFest experience, many of my overseas travels arose out of a solitary gig dating back to my days with Reunion Records. The company had been looking for someone to perform for a group of about forty people in Branson, Missouri. They'd asked almost every other artist on the roster when they finally came to me.

"Phil, would you be willing to do this gig?"

"What's the honorarium?" I asked.

"There is no honorarium. They can't put you up. They just want a good worship leader, and it would be great to have a relationship with them."

The label had brought this request to me, so I figured, *there must be an opportunity here.* I think I paid my own way, and I know for sure that I didn't make anything from it. The gig was for youth ministry directors from all over the country, and from that single performance I was asked to lead worship at a bunch of youth conventions.

Through those youth conventions, I met the head of missions for a large denomination. This man had actually seen me on *American Idol*—I think he was a missionary in Germany at the time—and he was now back in the US leading the whole operation. Soon I was being booked by missionaries all over the world.

By 2013, I was spending nearly four months a year overseas. I learned there was an entire world of pastors and ministry leaders out there who could benefit from the platform God had given me on *American Idol*. In many countries, my experience on *American Idol* was a huge drawing card. International ministries wanted me to sing "Blaze of Glory" at their events, and it was a hit. "Our community doesn't know Jesus," they said, "but they know 'Blaze of Glory.' They don't know Jesus, but they know *American Idol*." I discovered just how enormous the *Idol* platform was in other parts of the world.

Club Beyond, the military youth ministry of Young Life, recruited me to visit Europe on several occasions. I traveled to U.S. military bases, talking about topics like bullying and presenting the gospel. I spent several weeks in Europe each time, sometimes performing multiple gigs per day. I traveled with Trevor Hager, a musician who worked for me at the time and is like a brother to me. We did these journeys together like Paul and Silas, and it was fantastic.

I traveled around the world many times. Kendra and the girls sometimes met up with me overseas, and we all had a great time. The *Idol* experience was an important part of my life, but I was now doing what I loved, what I was called to do. Ministry and missions fulfilled me in a way that nothing else did.

When I wasn't traveling overseas, I performed on weekends and spent my weekdays with the family. I still sang at plenty of churches, but I wasn't working for one. And I couldn't have been happier.

CHAPTER 18

REACHING BEYOND

———

I WAS IN INDONESIA when I discovered that someone had it in for me. Thanks to my missions work, I was invited to do a concert in Jakarta—the largest city in the largest Muslim nation in the world. It's a country where there are still attacks against Christian churches. The manager of our hotel asked if he could take us out. We thought he was being hospitable, but he took us to a brothel, where the women were all over us.

"I'll pay for whatever you guys want," he said.

Of course we left, but it's pretty clear that we were singled out in Indonesia. The pastor who invited us told us afterward, "That guy knows why you're here. He's anti-church, and he would have it in the newspapers that you guys had done this. He's trying to do damage to the church."

I even got threats on Twitter from Muslim groups, saying, "Don't come back."

While we were there, pop star Bruno Mars was scheduled to appear on *Indonesian Idol*. (Yes, it's a popular hit show there, too.) But something happened that forced Bruno to cancel, so at the last minute they were scrambling to fill his role. Somebody who worked for *Indonesian Idol* attended the church that had invited me and made the connection: "Hey, there's an *American Idol* guy here in Indonesia." I ended up on the show, and they allowed me to promote my concert on Indonesian television.

Evangelism is technically illegal in Indonesia, but because I was on *American Idol*, they essentially let me invite the viewing audience to church. I sang a couple of songs, including "Blaze of Glory," then announced the concert and a website where they could find more information. The response was so overwhelming that we had to add a second night. We filled a 3,000-seat auditorium two nights in a row. It was awesome how we were able to share the gospel through this event.

In some countries it's completely okay to talk about the gospel; in some of them it's not. Almost every time, the reason I'm allowed to do so is *American Idol*. My history with the show supersedes the competing desire to keep the church out.

Between 2010 and 2013, I was able to sing and share the gospel with millions of people around the world. I sang at crusades. I sang at huge church events. I performed on radio shows and appeared on television.

Despite all of the trials, my time on *American Idol* paid off with so many great opportunities. In retrospect, if it all ended tomorrow, if I never got to perform again, I will always be grateful for how God used *American Idol* to open doors for me to share Christ with millions.

When Kendra told me during *Idol* that it wasn't all about me, that there were plenty of great singers out there, and that God had made all of it possible, she was absolutely right. We were both raised in homes where we were taught to believe that God has a purpose for your life. I think back to standing in my parents' driveway with a gun to my head, and I believe that God spared me for a reason.

One of my favorite ministries is Reach Beyond, a US missions organization that shares the gospel through radio. They have a real passion for what are known as "unreached people groups," and radio is a great way to reach people in their own language. One of their team members, a guy named Steve Johnson, approached me to see if I would perform a song called "Reach Beyond" for the organization.

The interesting thing about this project is that I wasn't their first choice; I just had the right name at the right time. One of Kendra's relatives, maybe a second cousin, worked with Reach Beyond and suggested me. She had heard some others, including Steve, talking about this song and trying to find someone to record it. They actually wanted to get legendary Christian artist Phil Keaggy, but she thought they'd said Phil *Stacey*.

"My second cousin is married to Phil Stacey," she mentioned.

"We're not talking about Phil Stacey," they replied, but then Steve spoke up: "Wait a second. I've met Phil Stacey."

I first met Steve at a publishing event several years prior. I sang a couple of songs and waved to the crowd, and afterward I went around the room shaking people's hands. One of those people was Steve. I didn't remember meeting him, but he remembered me, so he called and asked, "What would you think about doing this song?"

Steve and another guy from Reach Beyond came out to see me in Nashville, and we met at a restaurant near the Grand Ole Opry. "I'm down to help you in any way I can," I told them. "You contacted me at the best time possible, because I'm a missionary at heart. That's what I want to be doing right now, and I will absolutely record this for you."

"What's it going to take?" they asked.

"Don't pay me for this," I said. "I'm happy to do it for free, promote it for free. I'll do whatever you need."

A missionary from Thailand named Ty Stakes had written the original song, and Reach Beyond wanted me to record a more modernized version. I enlisted one of my music buddies named Chris August to help with the production. I first met Chris when I was on *American Idol*, and since then he'd won the 2011 Best New Artist award for Christian music.

We recorded the track at Chris August's home studio in

Nashville. He rewrote the music and recorded the band, and then I sang the vocal. When the song released, it made it to number eleven on the Christian chart.

———

Late in 2013, I was on a short Christmas tour with Chris Sligh from *American Idol.* One of our stops was a church in the Kansas City area, where they asked if I could fill in for their worship pastor on a Sunday morning.

Hold on a minute—hadn't I already been down this road before?

"What if they offered you a job here?" Kendra joked.

"I would sooner go to Syria than Kansas City again," I said. "And I never want to work for a church again."

Famous last words.

I agreed to fill in, and I had a great time. Sure enough, a few months later their regular worship pastor took another job in Seattle, which meant they had an opening. That's when the senior pastor, Matt Purkey, started calling to see if I would take the job. I said thanks, but no thanks.

I was already doing what I loved. I was traveling around the world; I was making good money; I was taking care of my family; I was having fun and doing well. We had a large house in Tennessee, and we were able to open our home to anyone who needed a place to stay. Taking this church job would mean a significant decrease in pay, and life as we knew it would change.

But this pastor wasn't one to give up easily. Matt called again right as I was leaving on a month-long tour for Club Beyond. He asked me to pray about the job offer while I was over in Europe—that if it was God's will, He would open my heart to it.

"I can see you're closed off to it," Matt said, "but you keep coming to mind when I'm praying."

I agreed to pray about it too, and after my time in Europe, I continued on to Japan. There I met up with some missionary friends, and I told them about the situation.

"I can't stop thinking about this church position," I said. "But I don't know that I want to work at a church again."

"We don't blame you," they said, "but have you prayed about it?"

"I'm praying about it now," I replied.

"Until God says go and you feel it in your soul, don't go."

At the time, Kendra and I were considering the possibility of relocating to Europe. Not only was I uninterested in full-time church work, I didn't want to go back to Kansas City. My missionary friends gave me good advice, yet as soon as they said it, I felt like God was leading me to take the position after all.

We left Tennessee for Kansas in the summer of 2014. I initially declined because God had me on the road with Reach Beyond and other missions organizations, but the church was really accommodating.

"Keep doing it," they said. "We'll send you out. You'll be a missionary from our church."

This time was a phenomenal season of ministry. My faith deepened as well as my understanding of theology. My relationship with God was growing stronger every day.

―――――――――

I didn't think I was ready to be a pastor, and I'm still not sure I was ready at the time, but I jumped in and loved it.

City Center Church has a couple thousand people, and I'm the creative arts pastor—the one who plans all the services. I'm involved with leading the staff in prayer, and I'm available to meet with church members.

Singing on Sundays is the easy part. I have an extraordinary group of worship leaders and singers and a band full of pro-level musicians who love Jesus. There's a sense of camaraderie and love for one another in my department that makes leading it an absolute joy.

My job would be easy if it was just about music, but that's not what being a pastor is about. Being a pastor means you get into other people's lives. They depend on you. When they have a tragedy, when they are in the hospital, when there's a death in the family—you are the person they call. I've been on the phone with parents who've lost children or grandchildren in horrible accidents. I'm on the phone with them the night it happens, and I'm at the funeral with them days later.

I coordinate all the creative elements of the service— music, baptisms, communion—but what really weighs on me is working with hurting people. I think most pastors feel that weight; and when our people are hurting, we often hurt with them. We want to help bear that weight.

So many of the problems we face in the church can feel superficial. I was so focused on the mission field because I wanted to do stuff that I thought was *important*. I had decided that the mission field was somehow more important than church work, and I was missing the point: There are hurting souls everywhere, not just overseas. The church is here to help them. The church is Christ's bride.

When I first came to this church, I told Matt, "I can see this lasting for around two years." I held on to my house in Nashville, and I probably tried to resign at least three times in the first few years. But whenever I tried to leave, I felt God speaking to me: *It's not time.*

Then, a couple of years ago, I sensed God encouraging me to plant roots at City Center Church. I hadn't put down real roots since I was a kid. Growing up in Ohio was the longest I'd ever lived in one place, and all of a sudden it felt like Kansas was home. When we first arrived, we were still planning on being missionaries. We'd even considered moving to Belgium. That was our plan, but God's been telling us, *You want a mission field to work in? Here's your field.*

CHAPTER 19

LOVE IS THE ANSWER

WE LIVE in an extremely consumer-based culture. Someone, somewhere, is always trying to sell us something, and it often seems that Christians have fallen into the same transactional mindset. As long as we attend church, sing along, listen to the sermon, and give our tithe, we think we're doing our part.

But it wasn't always like this. For much of Christian history, believers focused on sharing their faith and helping to make disciples. So how do you reach the culture when the culture has changed radically? How do you reach people with a radical notion—the gospel—that is offensive to those who don't believe? How can we effectively cast a net that will engage as many people as possible?

You don't catch fish by throwing a shark in the water; they'll all swim away. But if you dangle the right bait, the fish will come to you. If you want to be a modern-day fisher of men, what's the best lure?

That question has been asked for centuries, and the answer hasn't changed. The answer is love. Our job is to love people supernaturally. Jesus said it is by our love for one another that people would recognize we are children of God (John 13:35). How well we love one another and how well we love our communities should compel atheists to question their views. Jesus told us that the greatest commandments are summed up in loving God and loving others (Matthew 22:34-40). We don't talk enough about love.

This was the premise of Reach Beyond's "Bold" campaign: How do we truly love people who don't know Christ? Can we learn to care about everyone God cares about—not just the people living under our roofs, not just the people on our streets, but everyone? God desperately loves everyone. He sent His Son to die for everyone, including people who have never heard the gospel, and He wants us to share that message with boldness.

Steve Johnson invited me to host/narrate the "Bold" video campaign. It was a great project, and it helped me consider what it means to "make disciples" (Matthew 28:19). It reminded me of my own spiritual journey: I grew up in the church, but I truly fell in love with God on a mission trip to China in 1998. My *American Idol* experience taught me a lot about God's nature. I was twenty-nine years old when I really began to grasp the extent of His grace and who He is.

I love the idea of going to an unreached people group or an area where I can demonstrate the love of Christ. I hope people recognize me as someone who loves Jesus.

When I perform, I share my testimony about how God saved me from a carjacking, or how He provided groceries for me, or how my dad stepped in at Village Inn and mirrored my heavenly Father's love. I've learned that no matter the hardship I've endured, God's love is unfailing. He is there for me and He is there for you. Those are my three "go-to" stories, but I've got a million more.

There was the time when Kendra and I were taking our new baby's bed from Colorado to Oklahoma. It was a wooden crib in the back of a pickup truck, and it started raining. I prayed, "God, we really need this crib. Please let it stop raining." For an hour we saw rain in front of us and rain behind us, but I never had to use my windshield wipers.

Then there was the time I performed at a large Christian event in Pennsylvania. The organizer had no idea how to put a concert together, but he wanted to reach local high school kids for Jesus. He scheduled the event at an outdoor baseball park, and—to his surprise and shock—the stands were packed an hour before the event began. Suddenly it began to pour, and people started to leave. We stood on the stage and prayed that God would stop the rain, and it stopped immediately. About ten minutes after the event was over, we shut our car doors and it started raining again.

And there was the time I agreed to sing at a worship event in Michigan; I was also invited to sing at a guy's church that was on the route there. On the way to this extra gig, we discovered that we were not performing at a church. It was actually at someone's house—a small business owner who wanted me to sing for his workers. I started to stress a bit about the finances, so I bowed my head: *God, I pray that we get enough gas money to make it on this trip. Give us enough gas money.* I knew that the whole trip would probably cost me a couple of thousand dollars, and I told God that I would be satisfied with gas money.

When we were done playing, the business owner gave us a check that paid for the entire trip, and he gave each of my band members an extra bonus. He went above and beyond for us. And on my way out, as we were about to leave for the larger event, the owner stopped me. "God told me to do one more thing," he said. "He wanted me to fill your gas tank for you."

"You've already done plenty," I said.

"No, I'm going to obey God," he replied. "He told me to make sure I filled your gas tank."

For me, it's more evidence of God's love and His provision for the work He's called us to. When you follow Him, He takes care of you. Jesus talked about the lilies of the field and the birds of the air and how God feeds them and clothes them. How much more will He take care of us, His children? (Matthew 6:26-30)

When we step out in faith to do something for the Lord,

it's easy to be concerned about whether you'll have enough to pay the bills. When you work in ministry, you don't always get paid what you're hoping for. But God is always faithful. He always provides.

———

It's tough to keep from recounting all of the wonderful things God has done. I immediately think of my father-in-law, Mark McIntosh. He had some incredible encounters with God as a teenager, surrendered his life to Christ, and eventually became a preacher. Mark was pastoring a church in Wichita when I was in high school, and one night he came into my Village Inn location.

The manager put him in my section. By now I knew what I was doing, and Mark had such a positive experience that he became a regular at Village Inn. I had no idea who his daughter was yet.

Years later, when I first met Kendra, Mark was away on a business trip. The moment he saw me again, he remembered. "You were my server at Village Inn," he said. Before the night was over, he remarked, "Maybe when we're older you guys can get a house down the street from us. We'll live close to each other."

Little did he know.

My father-in-law is one of the best men you'll ever meet. He's filled with the love of Christ and love for his family— including me. The day I got married, right before I met

Kendra at the altar, Mark told me, "Just remember that I'm your biggest fan. I'll always be your biggest supporter."

He's backed up that statement ever since.

———

On July 4, 2017, Kendra received a frantic phone call from her mother, Tami. It was the middle of the night and we were staying at my parents' house in Tennessee. In just a few hours we were scheduled to board a plane out of Nashville, headed to Africa for a trip with Reach Beyond.

From what I could make out, it sounded like Tami was riding in an ambulance with Mark. Apparently Mark had been up late that night when he collapsed. Tami called for an ambulance, then she phoned Kendra.

Kendra, meanwhile, was going crazy. "What's wrong with Dad?" she asked.

I could hear Mark talking just fine. It certainly didn't sound like anything serious.

"He's going to be fine," I said. "Let's go to Africa."

My mother is a nurse, and by this point she was awake with us and listening for details.

"I can't really make out what happened," she said.

"Is it okay to go to Africa?" I asked.

Mom had a feeling: "Phil, don't go."

By daybreak we were getting more information. "It's an aortic dissection," Tami told us. When my mother heard that, she looked directly at Kendra. "You need to be prepared."

We had never heard of an aortic dissection, which occurs when the aorta splits. It sometimes kills the victim instantly; those it doesn't kill are often left paralyzed. We were about to load up our suitcases, but now we contacted Reach Beyond to say we couldn't make it.

Kendra, understandably, was freaking out. We booked a flight to Denver instead, and by the time we arrived, Mark was in bad shape. A few hours earlier he was talking on the phone, so it couldn't have been that bad—but it *was* that bad. We weren't sure if he was going to live.

The doctors said that Mark had lost the use of his legs and that they weren't sure how well the rest of the aorta would hold up. Only one layer of his aorta remained intact. Once the first layer tears, we were told, it usually just keeps tearing. The doctors did some sort of surgery, but most of the damage was already done.

It was a couple of weeks before Mark was fully conscious and aware, and that's when the doctor informed him, "You're not going to walk again." Mark gathered us around his bed. He took hold of Tami's hand and Kendra's hand, and he said, "I'm looking forward to seeing what God does with this." Then he prayed and praised the Lord.

We soon concluded that Mark and Tami couldn't remain in Colorado. Tami couldn't handle his care alone, so we decided to have them come live with us in Kansas. At the time, we lived in a little duplex in Overland Park. It was a great place and we loved it, but it certainly wasn't big enough for me and Kendra and the girls *plus* my in-laws.

We eventually found a house that was a perfect fit for our needs—an affordable home with six bedrooms, a three-car garage, and an elevator.

Looking back on Mark's life, God didn't shelter him from trouble, but when the trouble came, God prepared a way. God had provided for me so that I could help provide for Mark. God opened up a home where we all could live. Mark and Tami have their own section of the house, so they have privacy.

Mark remains in a wheelchair. He's okay to be home alone for a couple of hours, but he needs help with many tasks.

He now has a job working from home. Mark still sees God at work in his life, he prays every day, and he's wonderful to be around. Many people tell me, "Man, you're such a good guy for opening your house to your in-laws." I tell them that they have it backwards: "You guys have no idea how good this man has always been to me. It's an honor to care for him and for my mother-in-law."

I may not gamble, but I definitely won the in-law lottery.

———

My daughters and I are close now, but it wasn't always that way. The hardest period was after all those months on *American Idol*, since we'd spent so much time apart. I had to completely rebuild my bond with Chloe, who was only four years old at the time. McKayla, however, was still an infant. I learned to hold her as much as possible, even when she cried, until she finally loved being in my arms again.

Because I did so many concerts every year, the girls were homeschooled from a young age. By taking my family on the road with me, they've seen and done things that I never did growing up. We traveled for a while in a Dodge Caravan we nicknamed Big Bertha. It was a conversion van with a television that didn't work, and we had a blast driving across the country.

There are downsides, of course, when you're part of a touring family. The girls weren't able to build many relationships with people back home. Chloe had one friend her age in our neighborhood, so they hung out quite a bit when Chloe was younger, but McKayla didn't have anybody for a long while.

I used to justify all the time I spent on *Idol* by saying, "This is for my kids," but that was a bunch of baloney. I didn't know it was baloney at the time, because in my head I'd convinced myself that my kids would rather see their dad achieve his dreams than actually have him around. But that's not true—they would much rather have me with them.

The last year or so has been tougher financially because I haven't toured as much. I decided that my family needs me to be home. I had many offers before COVID-19 hit, and I'm confident that I'll be back on the road again someday. But lately I've wanted to focus on parenting, on being a good father.

We've been very open with our children about our past. They know about my mistakes—about my interactions, about being promiscuous, about smoking marijuana. They know kids who are smoking pot now, and I've sat my girls down for a talk. "I smoked pot," I said, "and I thought it was great because it made me feel good. But in the end it affected my life in a really negative way."

As a young man I made plenty of poor choices. I've come a long way since then, and I thank God for that. I've taken on the attitude, when I'm interacting with my girls, that I want them to walk away from each encounter with a deeper understanding of God as their heavenly Father. I want them to have a better picture of God through me, just like my wife should have a better picture of Christ through me. If I treat her with contempt or disrespect, I've ignored the Bible when it says for husbands to love your wives as Christ loved the church (Ephesians 5:25).

Christ loved the church so much that He gave Himself up for her. In the same way, I have to be willing to lay down everything for Kendra. I have to be willing to serve her. If we have disagreements, I have to make sure she knows, first and foremost, that "Phil loves me." My girls need to be certain of the same thing.

The challenge with kids is sustaining that sense of certainty. The challenge is to love your children even when you're frustrated or upset so that they never doubt *My Father in heaven must really love me!* I need to consistently model the love of God to my family.

I've pastored people for whom it took a long time to be able to call God "Father." Perhaps their human fathers were abusive or abandoned them. Perhaps they were just plain mean. I don't want my kids to look back at their childhood and say, "He was angry all the time. He was frustrated all the time. He didn't spend time with us. I can't envision God as a father because my own father wasn't there for me."

As inadequate as I often am, I want my family to have a positive image of God through me. They need to know that my love for them is unconditional. Unchanging. Unshakeable.

Love is indeed the answer.

CHAPTER 20

FOCUSING ON LIFE

———

YOUTH CULTURE has changed dramatically since I was young. When I was in high school, just about everyone knew about Jesus. They weren't all believers, but they knew something about the Christian faith. Since then I've worked with numerous young people, especially high schoolers, through organizations like Club Beyond. I even spent several months as an interim youth pastor. What those experiences taught me is how much has changed in the last twenty years.

For example, I visited one particular family because their daughter was a suicide risk. The mother wanted a social worker, and somebody recommended me.

When I showed up, she said, "Thank you so much for coming! I need a social worker."

"I'm a youth pastor," I replied, "so everything I say is going to be biblical."

"That's wonderful," she said. "I've always told my daughter to put God first."

I learned that the girl had sent a boy a nude selfie, which he then posted on the internet. The other kids ridiculed her, and she lost a lot of her friends. The girl was so troubled and distraught that the mother feared she would kill herself.

The first thing I said to the girl was, "What do you know about Jesus?"

"I know that people say His name as a cuss word."

She didn't know anything. Yet her mom had said, "I've always told my kids, God first." This girl was a straight-A student from a nice home in a good neighborhood, but she knew nothing whatsoever about the Bible. I didn't realize we'd regressed so far in the United States. It was important for me to see that.

I've learned that many girls in America have been pressured by young men to send explicit photos. Parents of teenagers need to know this, and my own girls have seen the consequences. We're living in a porn culture. So many boys are into pornography that they're not pressuring girls for sex as much; they're pressuring them for photos. Too many girls give in to that pressure because the girls who send photos are the ones gaining the boys' attention.

That's one of the things I talk about in public schools. One of the first times I addressed these topics in a public school setting was around 2012 in Chicago, on behalf of a local pro-life pregnancy center. My role was to talk to the students about teen pregnancy and sex education. There are a high number of teen pregnancies in the Chicago area, and the school system allowed me to perform and to talk about abstinence.

"Think about who you want to be, the person you want to be," I told them. "And make your decisions based on that—not based on what you feel like in the moment, because that moment will betray you."

The more I worked with young people and the more I spoke at high schools, the more I learned about issues such as bullying and suicide awareness. Then, a couple of years ago, I was approached by Focus on the Family to host the video portion of a new suicide-prevention training program called *Alive to Thrive*. Steve Johnson from Reach Beyond had started working for Focus on the Family, and he remembered the work I did on the "Bold" video series.

"I showed 'Bold' to the people at Focus," Steve said, "and they thought you'd be a good narrator."

Partnering with Focus on the Family to combat teen suicide was one more opportunity to care for hurting people, and it was a timely one. Teen suicide in my community was a massive problem—an epidemic. The week Steve contacted me about *Alive to Thrive*, we'd heard about three suicides at one high school in Kansas City. And the day I arrived in Colorado Springs for the video shoot, my daughter Chloe was contacted by a classmate.

"I'm done living," the girl announced. "I'm tired of this and I just wanted to tell you goodbye."

My daughter called me immediately. "Dad, what should I do?"

I'm in Colorado for the video, and I'm thinking, *How crazy is it that we're taping this right now?* I knew who the girl was—she attended our church—so I told my daughter: "You did the right thing. I'm going to call the youth pastor and he can reach out to her."

My work on *Alive to Thrive* helped me apply what I'd learned to my own family. I was able to speak honestly with my daughter and to engage in productive dialogue. "Honey, there's absolutely no shame in what you and your peers are feeling," I told her. "When I'm in a room full of students and I ask how many of them have had a suicidal thought, almost every hand goes up. Don't feel like you're abnormal; don't feel like everything's over because of this. Just know that there's a light at the end of the tunnel and you're going to make it through. And we're going to be here to help you, no matter what."

Several people I interviewed for the video stated clearly that if somebody close to them had known how to guide them through those feelings, they never would have attempted suicide. Over the years I've addressed students about bullying, sex, and social media—issues that lead some of them to suicide, but I realize I'm no expert. I still need to direct a troubled teen to someone with professional experience. What we can all do is help take away the stigma and assure young people that they *can* recover from having suicidal thoughts. I'm convinced that *Alive to Thrive* helps save lives.

———

Thanks to my involvement with *Alive to Thrive*, Focus on the Family invited me to participate in a massive pro-life rally with a similar name. "Alive from New York" took place on May 4, 2019, in the heart of Manhattan, featuring music, speakers, and—the highlight of the event—a live 4D sonogram of a third-trimester baby. The ultrasound images were displayed on giant video screens for the thousands gathered in Times Square and livestreamed to countless more watching online.

I cohosted the online portion of the event, which included interviewing speakers and performers backstage. I already knew more of the folks there than I expected—I've met singer Francesca Battistelli, and one of her musicians came from a church where I led worship—and it was great to see so many familiar faces. While I settled in behind the stage, the audience was already gathering and the protesters were already protesting.

The event was described as the largest pro-life rally in the city's history, and it was exciting to be part of it. It was also a little crazy. Planned Parenthood scheduled advertisements on the big screens around Times Square at the same time as the event, which was odd to see but not unexpected. We had the sense that we were making history that day, and I marveled at witnessing it firsthand.

In particular, I was struck by the passion of Alveda King, niece of famed civil rights leader Martin Luther King Jr. As Alveda took the stage, the first thing out of her mouth was the classic hymn, "There's Something about That Name." Not only did the audience sing along, but the protestors started paying attention. Alveda quoted her uncle's famous statement—"Injustice anywhere is a threat to justice everywhere"—and followed those words with a poignant question: "Where is the lawyer for the [unborn] baby?"

That's when I noticed some protesters on the fringes of the crowd lowering their signs. One woman in particular was crying. She stepped away from her fellow protesters and crossed the barriers that separated them from the pro-life audience. She asked for a pro-life sign, and she wasn't the only one. I watched several protesters join with pro-lifers at a rally they had come to oppose. Alveda King presented a powerful message, one that broke through ideological walls.

Imagine that you'd climbed out of bed in the morning, got dressed, made your sign, and showed up to protest this event, yet before it was over you'd joined the other side! I can't say that the thought process was the same for everyone, but I do know that Dr. King is obviously a legend in the civil rights movement, and seeing one of his relatives present a countercultural perspective on abortion—that it's an

attack on people of color, Black Americans in particular—
was a dramatic moment of clarity.

Who knows? Maybe they all picked up their signs and
protested somewhere else the next day, but that moment
made an impression on me. There's nothing like watching
someone's perspective transformed. To see minds changed
on such a divisive issue—literally a life-and-death issue—was
extremely powerful.

The main draw of the event was the chance to witness a
live 4D ultrasound on a giant screen. Since none of the Times
Square vendors would lease Focus on the Family space on
their digital billboards, Focus brought in three massive screens
on flatbed trucks. That enabled a pregnant Abby Johnson,
the former abortion-rights activist and Planned Parenthood
clinic director, to show New York—and the world—exactly
what kind of life the government refuses to defend.

Everyone with eyes could see a baby living inside Abby's
womb. Everyone with ears could hear her baby's heartbeat.
I've generally avoided live-broadcast events since my time on
American Idol, but this one was different. This one was special. It felt like we were involved in the Revolutionary War,
and we were all on the right side because we were fighting to
protect the lives of unborn children.

I'm not particularly political; I'm just a follower of Christ,
and I try to live at peace with everyone. But that's hard to do
in our day and age, when it seems like the moment you start
talking about your views you're ostracized by half the popula-
tion. I don't see abortion as a political issue as much as it is

a stain on humanity, an atrocity in our generation. There's truth in the statement that one of the most dangerous places for a child is inside the womb.

I know many people who see nothing wrong with abortion. I still love them, of course, and I won't call them names. And to anyone who's struggled with feelings of guilt because you've had an abortion, I want you to know that you are loved, that there is room at Christ's table for you, and that everyone can be forgiven.

─────

My trip back home began with your standard Uber ride to the airport. The driver was a Muslim, and somehow we started talking about faith. The conversation began when he asked me what I was doing in New York.

"We just held a giant pro-life rally," I said.

"Wow. Tell me about that," he said.

I told him that I was there with a Christian organization called Focus on the Family.

"Oh, you're a Christian," he said. "I respect that. I'm a Muslim." And that's how we got on the subject.

"Tell me about your family," I said. "Tell me about your life and background."

I was able to share the gospel with this driver. I've done ministry in Islamic areas around the world and I know the Quran pretty well. I've read it a few times. The differences between Christianity and Islam regarding the person of Jesus are fascinating to me. Talking about Jesus with Muslims is always refreshing to me because they revere Him too. They see Him as a great prophet.

For some reason the drive seemed to take hours, so we had plenty of time together. At one point he was crying. When we reached the airport, the driver got out of the car, hugged me, and gave me my money back from the trip.

"Oh, no," I said. "You have to let me treat you."

"You did treat me," he replied. So I allowed him to bless me.

This was not an isolated incident. Sharing my faith is one of the best things I get to do in life.

Death, whether through suicide or abortion or sickness, is a consequence of sin. Eternal life, meanwhile, is a gift from God (Romans 6:23). John 10:10 tells us that the enemy comes to steal and kill and destroy, but Christ came that we might have abundant life. I advocate for life because I want people to find the wonderful love of Jesus and the hope, joy, and peace that He offers.

If that means hosting an online video series or interviewing folks backstage in Times Square, I consider it an honor to assist in any way I can.

CHAPTER 21

LOVE EVERY HEARTBEAT

I REMEMBER WATCHING VIDEOS on the internet of quarantined Italians singing from their balconies. It was still early in 2020, and America had yet to enter any sort of lockdown, but I had a strong sense that the coronavirus was bound to hit us, too. Having spent so many hours on airplanes, I knew there was no way we could avoid the impact of COVID-19. And if the pandemic was inevitable, so was a quarantine. The concert and touring industries all but shut down, and many of my friends lost jobs.

Our church launched online services in March 2020, livestreaming Sunday mornings from the senior pastor's living room and Friday worship nights from my house. (One of my daughters usually operated a camera, while Kendra, I'm proud to say, is now an experienced video director!)

Right before our church's quarantine started, I added "pastor of groups" to my list of church responsibilities. My main goal was to make sure that people stayed connected. No big deal, right? The problem is, I've never been much of a groups guy. I'm still fairly introverted, and I get anxious sometimes when I'm with smaller groups of people. In the past I've joined small groups out of compliance or because I knew it was expected of me, but I've also looked for excuses to avoid them when I could. Yet the pandemic ended up teaching me a lot about the importance of small group ministry.

We began organizing online Zoom groups, and as the weeks went on, we built deeper relationships. We saw how the quarantine affected individuals, marriages, and families. We heard stories of loneliness, depression—even suicidal thoughts. We surrounded one another with prayer.

It was amazing to see the emotional and spiritual healing that took place. I ended up loving my small group. Our weekly meetings were definitely a highlight for me. I learned more about what it means to be the body of Christ. I witnessed firsthand how important it is that we stay connected. I often hear from other pastors how stressful ministry can be, and in many stressful situations (such as a pandemic) we tend to isolate ourselves. But times of stress are when we need each other more than ever. For encouragement. For prayer. For unity.

I tried to be extremely careful. I wore my mask and washed my hands. But it didn't stop me from catching the virus. I tested positive for COVID-19 in August 2020.

During the first few days of my sickness, Kendra and the girls were out of town. I didn't have the strength to drive myself to a testing center, but I knew it was the coronavirus. I had every symptom. Headache. Fever. Body aches. Cough. Exhaustion. Difficulty breathing. The only time I got out of bed was to assist my father-in-law. I was the only person there to help him, so I wore my mask, washed my hands fiercely, and avoided even talking in his direction.

My wife arrived home and took me in for a test. To no one's surprise, I received my positive results a couple of days later. Kendra took great care of me and, amazingly, no one else in the house caught the virus. Even after I was cleared by my local health department to return to work, I still kept my distance from everyone as a precaution.

My biggest project during this time was helping with the music for Focus on the Family's "See Life 2020" pro-life event. The event theme was "Love Every Heartbeat." Building on the success of 2019's "Alive from New York," the original plan was to hold live pro-life events in five different cities, but as the fall of 2020 drew closer and COVID-19 showed no signs of abating, everyone agreed that an online, virtual event was the way to go.

I helped recruit artists and songwriters to make the most

of the occasion. We scouted some great Nashville studio space in July, and we were scheduled to film the musical segments in early September.

Focus on the Family, of course, wanted me to provide a negative test result before I was cleared to enter the studio. They wisely wanted to protect everyone involved in the filming. So before I left for Nashville, I took another test to reassure everyone on the team that I was safe to participate. This time, however, the results didn't come back quite as quickly as my earlier tests. I decided to drive to Nashville anyway, hoping that the results would arrive before filming began.

They didn't.

Once I arrived, I let the crew know that my first test was still in process. That's when they sent me to a second, quicker testing center right there in Nashville. I was stuck outside of the studio while several of the other artists recorded their appearances. Finally, after another day of waiting, I received both of my pending results.

Both came back positive.

I was devastated. I sadly informed the team that I was unable to work on the project. Next, I contacted the health department to see why, if I was still positive, I had been cleared for work. I was told that traces of the virus would likely show in my system for months to come, even though I was no longer a transmitter. The Centers for Disease Control and Prevention (CDC) had apparently changed their guidelines, I learned, so that if an individual met certain benchmarks, including a specific number of days without symptoms, they could be cleared for work. In other words, I wasn't a risk. The film crew learned this as well, so we made the decision to proceed with recording my song—very carefully.

Instead of using the studio space we'd previously booked, the crew hauled all of their gear to a local church. (I was overwhelmed by the sacrifice on their part.) There, I was able to maintain a safe distance from everyone involved and still capture the event's signature song—a song I wrote with Michael Farren and Tony Wood. It was a deeply moving experience that I'll never forget, and I'll always be indebted to the people who went to extraordinary efforts so that I could participate in this wonderful event.

———

"Love Every Heartbeat" is perhaps the most special, heartfelt song I've ever been a part of. The goal was to communicate the value of every human life without expressing condemnation or judgment toward those with differing opinions. My original lyrics were a story-song about a girl who made the decision to keep her baby and found herself "loving every heartbeat," but it didn't quite feel personal enough. I called my friend Michael Farren to see if he could look it over and help me put the emotions and thoughts to paper. We scheduled a Zoom call and, to my joy, he invited Tony Wood—one of the best lyric guys in Nashville—to join us. Tony has written many beautiful songs, and if you listen to much Christian music, you've probably heard several of them.

The beginning of our conversation felt more like an interview. Michael asked, "Phil, what does your heart want to communicate?" and "Who is this speaking to?" Ultimately, I confessed my insecurity about writing the lyrics at all. Many women I know, especially those who aren't pro-life, don't want to hear a man's perspective on this sensitive issue. Sure, I've stated my position on abortion numerous times in interviews and church settings, but I really wanted to draw from my interactions with female friends who have come to me, trusting that I love them no matter what. These are women who faced a difficult choice and gave me the opportunity to share my heart with them. That, I said, is the emotion I wanted the song to express.

And that's when Michael started playing a beautiful chord progression. He began the lyrics with "This has never been an easy conversation. Since you're asking as a friend, here's what I'd say. . . ." I was immediately moved. From there the lyrics and melodies poured out of us fairly quickly. And what we produced was a special moment in the event.

This has never been an easy conversation
Since you're asking as a friend, here's what I'd say
I know you're scared, I know your world's been shaken
You're not the first to be here in this place

But that's the very best of you there on that screen
A story still unwritten, full of dreams

That heartbeat's gonna make memories
That heartbeat's gonna make you dance and sing
A life of precious moments yet to be
That heartbeat's gonna turn your world around
And that heartbeat's gonna make all of us proud
Imagine all the possibilities
When you love every heartbeat

I know right now you think that you can't do this
For sure not how you thought your life would go
But the truth is, no one's ever really ready
You just take a step and then before you know

You're staring into eyes that look like yours
A world of love you've never felt before

That heartbeat's gonna make memories . . .

I had first reached out to Michael in May 2020 to help me craft an anthem for the "See Life 2020" event—a "We Are the World" type of moment that gathered several artists together for a single song. Michael knows some great writers too, and they came up with so many amazing songs that we made the decision to record and include several of them in the program instead. Several Christian artists participated, and I'm honored to have been a part of this celebration of life.

It's important to me that we point people to Christ and not block their view of Him with our rhetoric. I oppose abortion, but I also know that it's legal in America. If you want to believe that abortion is a reasonable option for terminating a pregnancy, you have plenty of voices telling you that it is. Abortion advocates may consider me an enemy, but I don't consider them my enemies. I know everybody has their own personal experiences and worldviews, and those things shape how we view this issue. I try to keep that in mind when the topic comes up in conversation.

Soon after "See Life 2020" first aired online, I had a dream. In my dream, I was a presidential candidate participating in a big debate. Not surprising in a dream about politics, I was asked a question about abortion: "Do you want to see *Roe v. Wade* overturned?" My response in the dream took me a little by surprise, but I liked it: "I want to see *hearts* overturned."

_____

The year 2020 was crazy—from COVID-19 to murder hornets, from hurricanes to the election. But the thing that impacted me the most, at least on a personal level, was the conversation about racial injustice. This is another area where I'd like to see hearts changed. Racial injustice is a problem of the human heart. If I am submitted to Christ, I should consider others better than myself. I am to be a servant (Philippians 2:3-7). After all, Christ died for the sins of the *entire* world—male and female, young and old, black and white. He wants us to love every heartbeat, and black heartbeats matter.

There were many highly publicized deaths in the black community in 2020, and I have to confess that it was difficult to be a pastor in the midst of it all. I didn't witness overt racism growing up and I never heard racist comments in my home, but I was raised predominantly around white people. It wasn't until high school that I first noticed the lack of diversity in my life, though I didn't know what to do about it or how to address it.

When I left home for college, I didn't know much more than the basic history of the civil rights movement. No one taught me that Dr. Martin Luther King Jr. was killed before he could witness many of the changes he sought. When I listened to King's 1968 speech titled "The Other America," I better understood the differences between the world he grew up in and the one I grew up in. I began to notice the overwhelming whiteness of the restaurants where I ate, the grocery stores I patronized, the schoolteachers I had. I grew up in white America.

The country's racial divide became more evident when I arrived at Navy boot camp. Several of the black men in my division couldn't swim, so they had to take extra classes every week until they were able to pass a basic test. Passing the test wasn't a measure of athletic ability; learning to swim was a matter of childhood *opportunity*. I enjoyed summers at the beach and at swimming pools. They didn't. That meant they had to work twice as hard as I did in boot camp.

The racial divide was also evident on *American Idol*. In my experience, a white man who can sing well is seen as special, but a black man with a good voice is not that unusual. I watched several black men who were noticeably better vocalists get sent home. The only reason I could come up with is that *American Idol* was selecting a cast, and it couldn't be 100 percent black. I don't think the producers were racist—I just think they were trying to cast a diverse show.

The divide was even evident on tour. I've dined out with a lot of black singers, musicians, and speakers, and my beverage glass was frequently refilled while they had to repeatedly ask for refills. I watched people hold a door open for me, only to release it as one of my black counterparts approached. This sort of behavior certainly isn't universal, but I've seen it firsthand.

One of the friends who lived with us for a time in Kansas City is a black man who worked at a shopping mall down the street. He didn't have a car at the time, so he usually walked back and forth to work. I'll never forget the day I heard a truck horn honking at him as he entered our house in tears—the truck driver yelling obscene racial slurs. Many people I know think racism is dead. They're wrong. It may be fading, but it's still alive.

My circle of friends is much more diverse nowadays, and many of them are hurting. The last couple of years have been exhausting for them. They grew up in The Other America. They know it still exists. What's difficult for me is watching some people on social media try to tell them they're wrong.

I'm not black, so I can't tell you what it's like to be black in America. But I can sure listen to you when you tell me. I can trust you and the friendships we've built. I can demonstrate that I care by being there for you, by refusing to accept the status quo if it harms you or diminishes your dignity in any way. I don't think that's a political issue. That's a human being issue.

This moment in history is a significant opportunity for the church. Jesus said that His followers would be known by our love for one another. What a chance to show the world what Christlike love looks like! After all, we are members of the same body. We belong to one another. If my hand is hurting, I'm going to do whatever I can to help it heal; I'm not going to simply ignore the pain. In the same way, I believe the church can help lead the drive for racial unity. We have to accept responsibility for past failures and figure out how to better love our brothers and sisters. To build real, lasting friendships. To be more like Jesus.

We've seen tremendous progress in this area in our church. It's my desire to promote a spirit of unity as we work to worship God together with one voice. My latest musical project is called City Center Worship, and the goal is to use my platform to promote harmony—spiritual harmony, racial harmony, you name it—within the body of Christ. I want to see believers everywhere join together in unified worship, just as Jesus prayed for the unity of believers in John 17.

God commands us to love our neighbor. That means *every* neighbor, not just the ones who think and look and behave like us. He gives life to each heartbeat—the lonely heart feeling isolated by a pandemic, the newly formed heart of an unborn baby, and the hearts that beat inside my black brothers and sisters. Love is the key; it's how others will identify us as Christ's disciples. As Christians, we are called to love . . . to *love every heartbeat.*

CHAPTER 22

MADE TO WORSHIP

———

MY LIFE HAS BEEN AN INCREDIBLE JOURNEY. I've seen and done
so many amazing things that I sometimes have a hard time
believing it myself. I'm still surprised that I ended up on *The
Tonight Show* or *Ellen* or any of those other television programs. In retrospect, however, I can see God's hand in all of
it. I can see how He's led me to where I am today, but it was
often a confusing ride.

Each stage of my journey is one more chapter in a much
bigger story. From Kentucky to Ohio to Kansas; from college
to the Navy to *American Idol* to ministry—they all feel like
different lifetimes. When I say my time on *Idol* feels like it
took place in another dimension, I'm absolutely serious. This

is probably the first time in a decade that I've thought about many of the stories I've recounted in this book.

A few years ago, Kendra and I were sitting on the couch watching television, which is something we're rarely able to do. It was so rare, in fact, that it actually felt like a special occasion. It seemed so different, so unusual, that I told Kendra, "This is the first conscious moment when I've really been able to reflect on what's happened to us."

This was several years after *American Idol*, after years of touring and record deals and ministry around the world. That moment on the couch felt like the first chance we'd had to stop and catch our breath, to look at each other and simply say, "My goodness."

We were finally back to normal, whatever normal is for us. It was an opportunity to pause and reflect. Until then, life was so fast-paced. I went from *American Idol* to country music to Christian music to missions, and it all seemed like a blur.

I no longer stay at five-star hotels, but I'm certainly not ready to slow down. Sure, I'm a full-time pastor at a church, and God hasn't told me that I'm leaving, but I know from experience that seasons can change, and change drastically. I have absolutely no idea where I'll be a year or two from now, but in the meantime, I love my church, and I love the people. I like to think that I'll stay there as long as I can.

I'm starting to write music again. I hadn't written much for a few years, but I've been in the studio a lot more recently. There's still more music in me, and I'd like to release some of it before I'm done. Most of what I'm writing is for my church; however, I could also see myself performing these new songs at festivals and conventions. At one point I never wanted to see my name in lights or on posters, but God convicted me. *I gave you your name. I gave you the platform. You need to use that.* So I'm trying to be a good steward of the platform God's given me.

When it comes to other opportunities, events where I can stand for Christian values, I'll jump right on board. I'm especially passionate about the sanctity of life and suicide prevention. We're currently in a time of great division in the United States, so I'd like to see the church lead the way in bringing people together. My goal is to organize nights of worship in cities all over the country, to provide venues where believers can pray together and sing together and celebrate what God is doing in a spirit of unity. Jesus Himself prayed that we would be unified as one, just as He and the Father are one (John 17:20-23).

Remember how I struggled with the idea that some of the people I met in Hollywood were more loving than those I met in church? I eventually realized how unimportant it is to worry about how other people behave and whether or not they accept me. What's much more important is my own behavior, whether or not *I* am following Christ. I learned to focus on *His* voice, to study *His* Word.

That Hollywood experience taught me a lot about loving my neighbors. As for that "hate mail" I received after *Idol*, the Holy Spirit helped me not only to move past it, but eventually to heal from it.

Nowadays, as a pastor myself, I try to be slow to speak and slow to anger. And I definitely trust, a little more than I may have before, how God is working in the individuals I serve. After all, I've been there.

━━━━━━

Kendra started law school in the fall of 2019. My wife is the brilliant one, the president of just about everything she's a part of. After college she decided that she wanted to be at home with our kids, so we committed to that. We committed to that even before *American Idol*. When I was in the Navy, she was at home with Chloe. We made it work. After God opened the doors for *American Idol*, we had enough money to run our household and do what we needed to do. When I was touring, Kendra went on the road with me and home-schooled our kids.

Recently our girls decided to attend traditional schools, which meant Kendra felt free to take on a new role, a new responsibility. She's always looking for justice—which is why she gravitated toward the law. She took the LSAT once and scored extremely well, landing her a spot in law school almost immediately. She's already president of the university's Women in Law organization, and she's also a student ambassador who helps show new law students around the campus.

Law school is a challenge, and Kendra wanted a new challenge. I can see her doing anything she wants. She could be a senator one day. She could lead a firm dedicated to helping people.

Kendra is an extraordinary woman. She's extremely smart and strong, and I'm very proud of her. My role now as a husband is to support her, to get behind her and reduce her stress on the home front.

Since that night in Italy when I confessed to Kendra, we have been a committed husband and wife. We love each other unconditionally. Issues that would probably be more dramatic in some other marriages don't seem like a big deal anymore. Once you've had to overcome feelings of abandonment and betrayal, once your spouse knows you were in a hotel room with another woman and walked away, you have to rebuild a new level of trust. We have a new level of camaraderie and friendship. We're rooting for each other.

The same way we learned to work together with the Lee Singers back in college, we know how to work together today. When I'm out on the road, for example, Kendra helps run my business. She's great at it, and it gives me peace of mind. The arrangement began after I left the commercial music industry, because I never again want to experience what it feels like to owe hundreds of thousands in bills that I don't know about.

Nowadays, everything that comes against us seems so small. Even when we're working through family hardships like a child with a broken heart or a father-in-law going through a life-threatening episode, we always manage to handle it. I don't know how to explain it except that our marriage is blessed—that two individuals who came into marriage with completely different mentalities have learned to operate as one.

<hr>

When people ask me if they should audition for a singing competition like *American Idol* or *The Voice*, I tell them they need to understand what they're doing. I think you should do it in the same way that I think you should skydive some time in your life. Skydiving is fun, but it's also terrifying, at least the first time. *American Idol* was fun, but it was also traumatizing. There were special moments: For example, there was the time when Quincy Jones spent a couple of hours with just me and his daughter. I doubt he knows who I am today, but that day he did. And I'll never forget when Jennifer Lopez told me that my singing gave her goosebumps. Those people are all big stars, so it felt good when they were kind to someone like me.

At the same time, I walked away from *Idol* with a big hole inside of me. Not because of all the crazy stuff that happened, but because I realized that I'd fulfilled a dream and yet felt emptier than before. Dreams are like a hole that you desperately want to fill. *If I can achieve that, then this hole will be filled,* you reason. And then you finally reach that goal, but the hole is still there. It's still empty. I think that was the unanimous experience for the contestants on *American Idol.*

Hardly anyone gets a big career from these shows anymore. In fact, it's just the opposite. It's like they put a stamp on your face that you never want to be a star. The artists who are the most successful now are the ones who didn't make it. Colbie Caillat auditioned for *American Idol*; she didn't make it. Lauren Daigle auditioned for *American Idol* three times; she never made it past the Green Mile. Tori Kelly auditioned for *American Idol*; her journey ended the same way. And today she's a star.

It makes you wonder, *What's the point? What's the point of pursuing my dreams?* This is why *American Idol* has psychologists on the set, because the contestants walk away from it with a sense of defeat, an enormous feeling of loss. I'm not sorry that I did *Idol*, because my time with the show has shaped my life in many ways and has given me so many opportunities in ministry. But I had no idea what I was in for. I know of one finalist who didn't land a deal, and he had trouble getting out of bed for the next nine months. He thought his life was going to change, and all of a sudden . . . nothing. One day you're hanging out with Rihanna, and the next your phone isn't ringing. He just crawled into bed and stayed there.

Trying to figure out *what* happened—or didn't happen— can drive you mad. Pondering *why* only makes you sad. I've never met anyone who walked away from fame who later said, "I'm so glad I was famous." I do know a lot of famous people today, and most of them have gone through severe addictions or emotional struggles or multiple affairs. It seems as if fame is bad for the soul, yet we rarely talk about it because we assume that it's great to be famous.

Once I discovered that I didn't want fame, I stopped fighting for it.

━━━━━━━

Music was my life for many, many years, but it's no longer my passion. If I'm making an eight-hour drive from, say, Kansas City to Colorado, I rarely listen to music. I typically listen to the Bible, or if I do turn on music, it will be a worship experience. I still have my classic '70s playlist, but I'm no longer looking for the best new talent; I'm not searching for that thrill.

American Idol was an important part of my life—it changed everything at the time—but I credit most of what happened to the hand of God. And look at what He did through it. That's what amazes me.

More than 100,000 people auditioned for season six of *American Idol*, but somehow I made it to the finals. I signed a record deal with Lyric Street Records, a subsidiary of Disney. I signed a second record deal with Reunion, a subsidiary of Sony Music. I performed alongside famous music stars and shared the gospel with millions. *American Idol* certainly gets some credit for that, but I don't think it was all *American Idol*. I believe God opened doors and moved mountains. He had a sovereign plan.

So why should I tell others not to audition? If you want to do it, do it. It's a once-in-a-lifetime experience, and there are some enjoyable aspects. To this day, many people still know me as that *American Idol* guy. Even with my beard, I'm still recognized in airports. Or maybe I'll pay with a debit card and somebody recalls my name. "Wait a second. . . ."

That actually happened recently in Dallas. The woman had attended my high school, albeit years later, and she saw my card. "Are you Phil Stacey, the guy who was on *American Idol*?" People still get excited about it. It's more fun now because it's not about fame, it's not people ambushing you on the street. Nowadays they just want to say hello. "Oh my goodness!" they'll say. "What are you up to?"

"I'm a pastor at a church," I tell them.

When I say I'm a pastor, the usual response is, "That's really cool." I rarely get a negative reaction. People have even said, "It would be interesting to discuss faith with you, because I'm an atheist. I'd like to hear your perspective."

I love those conversations. I love those people because God loves those people. I want to hear what they have to say, because I want to introduce them to Jesus.

I still think about the woman who wrote to me when I was on *American Idol*—the Navy wife whose marriage was falling apart and who noticed the on-camera connection between me and Kendra. Her message moved me in a way that few could. *Even when I am at my worst, God is still able to use me!* How liberating is that? It takes all the pressure of performing off of my shoulders. It clarifies my purpose. My mission isn't to entertain people or manipulate them through the power of my vocal prowess. It's to bring glory to God.

I'm no longer a singer. I'm a worshiper. In fact, I was made to worship. When I place what little I have in God's hands, He takes it, blesses it, and uses it far beyond my wildest expectations.

The same can be said for every believer. Your purpose is not your favorite activity or what you do for a living. If that were true, then according to Acts 18:3, the apostle Paul's purpose would be making tents! When I was on *American Idol,* I learned that when your identity is wrapped up in the way others perceive you, insecurity and pride will most certainly follow. Those things can eat away at your life until they destroy you.

Genuine freedom comes when you discover that your primary purpose is to bring glory to God (Isaiah 43:7). We were created to worship Him. Whether you're a singer, nurse, teacher, server, engineer, or plumber; whether you're a husband, wife, father, or mother—do it all for the glory of God (1 Corinthians 10:31). Let Him take care of the rest.

I often remind people that God is not just a powerful God, He's also a good God. Every good and perfect gift comes from Him (James 1:17). As someone who leads others in congregational worship, I encourage people to use music as an opportunity to tell God how much we love Him. After all, music is one of His favorite things! It doesn't matter whether you consider yourself a good singer; no one else can offer *your* song to the Lord.

The next time you have the opportunity to worship Him, don't let anything stand in your way. Heartfelt worshipers don't need the catchiest melody or the greatest musicians—they just need an opportunity. Embrace the idea that the God of heaven, the keeper of joy and peace, craves your song. Stand up and remind yourself, *I was created for this. I was made to worship.*